D0874054

ALONG CAME GOOGLE

Along Came Google

A History of Library Digitization

Deanna Marcum and
Roger C. Schonfeld

PRINCETON UNIVERSITY PRESS

PRINCETON AND OXFORD

Copyright © 2021 by Princeton University Press

Princeton University Press is committed to the protection of copyright and the intellectual property our authors entrust to us. Copyright promotes the progress and integrity of knowledge. Thank you for supporting free speech and the global exchange of ideas by purchasing an authorized edition of this book. If you wish to reproduce or distribute any part of it in any form, please obtain permission.

Requests for permission to reproduce material from this work should be sent to permissions@press.princeton.edu

Published by Princeton University Press
41 William Street, Princeton, New Jersey 08540
6 Oxford Street, Woodstock, Oxfordshire OX20 1TR

press.princeton.edu

All Rights Reserved

Library of Congress Control Number 2021940432
ISBN 978-0-691-17271-2
ISBN (e-book) 978-0-691-20803-9

British Library Cataloging-in-Publication Data is available

Editorial: Peter Dougherty and Alena Chekanov
Production Editorial: Jill Harris
Jacket Design: Layla Mac Rory
Production: Erin Suydam
Publicity: James Schneider and Amy Stewart

This book has been composed in Adobe Text and Gotham

Printed on acid-free paper. ∞

Printed in the United States of America

10 9 8 7 6 5 4 3 2 1

CONTENTS

ACKNOWLEDGMENTS

This book had a long gestation period, and Peter Dougherty and the staff of Princeton University Press supported us throughout. Instead of complaining about our failure to meet milestones, they offered encouragement. Instead of critiquing what we submitted in early drafts, they offered additional ideas for our consideration. We count ourselves sublimely fortunate to have had an opportunity to work with Peter. We are also grateful for the excellent reviewers he found for our manuscript. They, too, offered great ideas for strengthening our arguments, and the result is a greatly improved work.

We acknowledge at the outset that we have played a part in many of the events we chronicle in this book and have been friends and colleagues of many of the key figures. Deanna Marcum has served in leadership roles at the Council on Library Resources, the Council on Library and Information Resources, the Library of Congress, and Ithaka S+R. Roger Schonfeld has been with the Andrew W. Mellon Foundation and ITHAKA for his entire career, currently serves on the board of the Center for Research Libraries, and wrote the history of JSTOR. Although we have tried to remain impartial tellers of this story, we recognize that our professional histories no doubt color our perspectives.

The real strength of this history is that so many key figures in book digitization were willing to talk with us so candidly. We are forever grateful to our colleagues and friends who made time to tell us how they experienced the early days of digitization and to reflect on the implications for scholarly communication, broadly considered. This book is the story of those pioneers: Alan Adler, Ivy Anderson, Heather Christenson, Dan Clancy, Dan Cohen, Paul Courant, Robert Darnton, Laine Farley, Dale Flecker, Mike Furlough, Kevin Guthrie, Brewster Kahle, Michael Keller, Paul LeClerc, Tom Leonard, Mark Sandler, Richard Sarnoff, Donald Waters, and John Price Wilkin.

We are also grateful to our many colleagues who talked with us about the framework for the book, the positions we have taken, and their thoughts about the implications of book digitization. That list of valued friends is too long to acknowledge all of them properly, but we owe special thanks to Clifford Lynch, Lorcan Dempsey, Jessica Gardner, Kevin Guthrie, and Oya Rieger for taking time to talk again and again about our work.

Thousands of individuals, far too many to name, contributed to the initiatives discussed in this study. And many more digitization experiments were pursued than we could cover in this project, even though we fully recognize that so many projects made important contributions. Each library that launched a digital project helped build the digital future. We owe an apology to the great number of librarians, technologists, and publishers who made invaluable contributions to book digitization whom we have not discussed in this book.

Finally, we are grateful to one another. When we first discussed this manuscript with Peter, he reminded us that it is not easier to write a book with a coauthor. In fact, he said, it is probably harder. For us, it has been an invaluable example of how collaboration can work. We remain good friends at the end of this long process, and we are convinced that our joint project is better than what either of us could have produced individually.

ALONG CAME GOOGLE

Introduction

On January 3, 2020, the *Washington Post* published a story about two graduate students working to save the University of Virginia's card catalog. Literature doctoral candidates Neal Curtis and Sam Lemley learned that the four million cards in the library's catalog that had not been updated in two decades would be discarded to make way for a massive renovation of Alderman Library. All the library's current holdings were included in an online digital catalog, so the outdated card catalog was understandably used by very few. Library administrators had determined that, at a cost of $750,000, it would not be worthwhile to scan the cards and create a digital surrogate of the outdated catalog. Instead, it seemed sensible to discard the card catalog, as so many other libraries have done since the 1970s when libraries began to create machine-readable descriptions of their collections instead of creating iconic cards that represented each book in the library. The dedication of the two graduate students prompted volunteers to help pack the catalog cards into 798 boxes and store them in an off-campus facility.

They have bar coded each box for retrieval so that students and faculty will be able to recall a box of cards and look at the entries and notes about specific books. This charming story of students volunteering to pack boxes to preserve what Sam Lemley described as "an accurate, preserved-in-amber view of what the library was in the twentieth century" is a good introduction to the current challenges: what will be the library of the future?

The Virginia students recalled a time when the university library built a collection of books that served the needs of scholars and students. But the university librarian, John Unsworth, faced a new set of challenges that propelled him to raise money for and undertake a massive renovation of the library. Part of the challenge was to bring the building up to fire, safety, and accessibility codes, but a much bigger challenge was that most students and faculty wanted more than print collections from the library. They wanted access to the galaxy of information resources that exist not only at the University of Virginia and but also everywhere else, not just in print form but digitally as well. There is no card catalog for today's information universe.

The end of the twentieth century and beginning of the twenty-first marked the transformation of libraries from builders and preservers of collections to information nodes that connect information seekers with resources from all over the world. This book focuses on what is perhaps the signal milestone in that transformation: the entry of Google into the library arena with promises of making all the world's information available to everyone.

With news of Google's plans, a shock wave went through the academic library community. Some librarians, eager to see an acceleration of digital activity, embraced the concept of a universal digital library and began advocating for change.

Others argued that librarians were experts in locating and validating information resources; they did not appreciate other players moving into their domain. At its core, the Google digitization project challenged the definition of "library." A large literature has developed over the past decade in the field of "Google studies," with scholars seeking to examine the effects of consumer technology companies, pursuing a combination of business growth and societal disruption. Within this field, there are many episodes where Google dipped its toes into a new sector and left an entire ecosystem spinning in disruption. Our goal in this book is not to offer a final judgment of Google but rather to explore deeply one example of its efforts to target an information space, in this case the important legacy of published materials held by libraries, and the results on an existing sector and ecosystem.[1]

Ultimately, the rapid change in user expectations and professional expertise with digital technology led to intense conversations within the library and academic communities about

---

1. See, for example, Siva Vaidhyanathan, *The Googlization of Everything (And Why We Should Worry)* (Berkeley: University of California Press, 2012); Ken Hillis, Michael Petit, and Kylie Jarrett, *Google and the Culture of Search* (New York: Routledge, 2013); Ken Auletta, *Googled: The End of the World as We Know It* (New York: Penguin, 2009); Amy Langville and Carl D. Meyer, *Google's PageRank and Beyond: The Science of Search Engine Rankings* (Princeton: Princeton University Press, 2012); Jean-Noël Jeanneney, *Google and the Myth of Universal Knowledge: A View from Europe*, trans. Teresa Lavender Fagan (Chicago: University of Chicago Press, 2007); and Elad Segev, *Google and the Digital Divide: The Bias of Online Knowledge* (Oxford: Chandos, 2010); as well as broader treatments such as Safiya Umoja Noble, *Algorithms of Oppression: How Search Engines Reinforce Racism* (New York: New York University Press, 2018); Christian Vandendorpe, *From Papyrus to Hypertext: Toward the Universal Digital Library* (Champaign: University of Illinois Press, 2009); Shoshana Zuboff, *The Age of Surveillance Capitalism: The Fight for a Human Future at the New Frontier of Power* (New York: PublicAffairs, 2019); Evgeny Morozov, *To Save Everything, Click Here: The Folly of Technological Solutionism* (New York, PublicAffairs, 2013); and Jaron Lanier, *Who Owns the Future?* (New York: Simon and Schuster, 2013).

the roles and responsibilities of both libraries and corporate entities, but meaningful organizational change in academic libraries was slower. The story of Google's digitization ambitions telescopes the dramatic changes in libraries, readers' research habits, and, perhaps, even reading itself.

Research libraries in particular came under pressure to adapt to this emerging reality. The notion that any library, no matter how large, could collect comprehensively the knowledge that was being produced was clearly not possible. With digital technology, many of the quality control mechanisms that had been in place for decades, for example, peer review of both journal articles and books through publishers with established reputations, now had to compete with preprints, open access publications, and start-up publishers with an array of review practices (some of them predatory). Libraries, no longer focused on collecting the best of the published record, began to think of their mission as wayfinding for their users. What is the universe of material on a particular topic? How does the reader find out about it?

In the midst of this transition from collection building to providing information services, Google made its dramatic announcement that it planned to digitize published books, which would be discoverable along with the websites Google was rapidly adding to its search capability. It knew, in a way that many others would only later recognize, that the layers of gatekeeping needed to produce publications and for the great research libraries to collect them would add significantly to the quality of the information available online.

In some respects, the Google project to digitize millions of books might have relieved research libraries of their stewardship responsibilities for legacy collections, allowing them to make the transition to digital libraries more quickly. But at least some librarians and a few scholars hesitated to entrust a corporation with digital library development. The story we tell here is how Google attempted to enter, and in some senses disrupt, the traditional scholarly communications systems that served the universities, their scholars and students, and their libraries for decades. We describe the competing forces that bolstered or fought against Google's efforts, as well as the fallout after the Google book digitization project fell into a legal quagmire. Finally, we describe the attempts to achieve some of the goals of the Google book digitization project in other ways and speculate about other possible scenarios that will benefit the scholarly community.

Looking back on the development of mass digitization and the efforts to thereby unlock access to our legacy of published books, it is clear that while many individuals and organizations played vital roles, none was more significant than that of Google. Even though the project that resulted and the impacts that it had were ultimately limited relative to the vision, millions of books have been digitized, the information they contain was made more discoverable, and access to many of them improved dramatically.

Google was able to lead because it was bold and agile. Larry Page had been interested in digitizing books since his student days at Stanford in the late 1990s. In 2002, he and Marissa Mayer determined that it would take forty minutes to digitize a three-hundred-page book. At-scale progress began to be realized when Dan Clancy was appointed to head the digitization project for Google. The team soon developed partnerships with publishers and then large research libraries in the United States, the United Kingdom, and several other countries. Paul Courant, the university librarian and former provost at the University of Michigan, and his colleague John Price Wilkin, then Michigan's associate university librarian, would provide especially important leadership for both the library digitization efforts and later preservation initiatives.

For nearly a decade, Google and its partners aggressively pursued the dream of a digital universal library. When, on March 22, 2011, the U.S. District Court for the Southern District of New York rejected the legal agreement that had been proposed by Google after being sued by publishers and authors, the utopian library fizzled into little more than dreamy aspirations.

Looking back on the failed agreement in 2017, *Atlantic* journalist James Somers reflected on what had been lost:

> You were going to get one-click access to the full text of nearly every book that's ever been published. Books still in print you'd have to pay for, but everything else—a collection slated to grow larger than the holdings at the Library of Congress, Harvard, the University of Michigan, at any of the great national libraries of Europe—would have been available for free at terminals that were going to be placed in every local library that wanted one.[2]

But this highly desirable digital library was not realized. Somers wrote, "When the most significant humanities project of our time was dismantled in court, the scholars, archivists, and librarians who'd had a hand in its undoing breathed a sigh of relief, for they believed, at the time, that they had narrowly averted disaster."[3]

---

2. James Somers, "Torching the Modern-Day Library of Alexandria," *Atlantic*, April 20, 2017, https://www,theatlantic.com/technology/archive/2017/04/the-tragedy-of-google-books/523320/.

3. Ibid.

The library community was not as monolithic as Somers seems to suggest. For some portion of librarians, at least, for some scholars, and for some futurists, the Google project promised a vision that they had been dreaming of for years. For the advocates, the Google book digitization project was the strategy for libraries.

For several decades, multiple individuals and organizations have seen book digitization as the best strategy for creating a universal library. This is our analysis of how the Google book digitization project developed, how other organizations and individuals responded to the advent of large-scale book digitization, and the implications for libraries, publishers, and the scholarly community.

———

Google's dream of a universal library was a technology-centric version of an old idea. Throughout history, scholars, librarians, and others who yearn for knowledge and learning have dreamed of building a comprehensive library that is accessible to all. The Great Library of Alexandria, beginning in 288 BC, aspired to collect all of the papyrus scrolls that had been written. The Ptolemaic rulers intended the library to be a collection of all extant knowledge. They sent agents to many different places to purchase as many texts as they could. Because Alexandria was a port city, they searched incoming ships for texts and made copies of them for the library.[4] In modern times, the great research libraries such as Harvard, the British Library,

———

4. Roy MacLeod, "Introduction: Alexandria in History and Myth," in *The Library of Alexandria: Centre of Learning in the Ancient World*, ed. MacLeod (New York: I. B. Tauris, 2004), 1.

and the Library of Congress, at least until recently, described themselves as "libraries of record," and they aspired to collect as much of the important scholarly and cultural record as possible.

As academic research expanded after World War II, publishing exploded, and libraries realized they could never acquire all that would interest their readers. Yet, the technological revolution inspired a great many library leaders to imagine how they would transform their organizations into the "universal library." In the 1960s, Library of Congress giants William Welsh and Henriette Avram believed that the enormous bibliographic database of that institution would become the core of the universal electronic library. Later, OCLC founder Frederick Kilgour would argue that a network of institutions could do that job more effectively. Computer scientists would question if we needed librarians at all if we focused instead on computational power to provide access to the entire corpus of knowledge.

But the digital transformation of our economy and society in recent decades has given rise to unbearable tensions— between global and hyperlocal, between universal access and filter bubble, between freedom and control, between openness and truth. During the industrial age, the library served as one of the greatest democratizing forces in American society. The network of public and research libraries was built on an aspiration (even if inequitably achieved) for any book to be available to any American without payment, yielding rich rewards for the economy and citizenship. A similar model for libraries was adopted in a number of other countries as well. And, no less than publishers and journalists, libraries too have been forced to wrestle with the tensions of the digital transformation.

Past generations of librarians focused on the needs of their own communities—their students and faculty members, not only those of the present but those of the future, in the case of the academic research libraries that feature prominently in our story. They spent handsomely to develop their collections, pushing aspirationally toward comprehensiveness in many cases, to provide access for local constituencies.

At the same time, they recognized that it was not possible to meet all of the research needs of their scholars and from the late nineteenth century began building sharing networks that made the academic library not a stand-alone provider but part of a network linked by lending. The pressure on research libraries to provide timely and comprehensive access to scholarly resources grew dramatically with the onset of World War II as the federal government became much more interested in the nation's scholarly capacity in a global environment.[5]

To achieve this end, libraries have developed mechanisms for building what Lorcan Dempsey has called a collective collection.[6] They have shared information about their collections with one another as a mechanism for coordinating their collecting activity. They developed a robust, frequently used, and increasingly streamlined interlibrary loan system to provide access to one another's holdings.

But, ultimately, libraries have responded more to local needs than national imperatives. And, perhaps more importantly,

---

5. For example, even as individual research libraries aspired to vastly increase the local collections available to their scholars, key academic and library leaders met in Farmington, Connecticut, to find ways to ensure a network of libraries from which the entire scholarly community could draw. The Farmington Plan ultimately failed after long years of trying, but it is the best example of how the dream of comprehensiveness would shift from the individual library to a "collective collection" shared across the libraries on behalf of their users. Ralph Wagner, *A History of the Farmington Plan* (Boston: Scarecrow Press, 2002).

6. Lorcan Dempsey, "The Collective Collection," August 5, 2005, https://www .lorcandempsey.net/orweblog/the-collective-collection/.

US libraries have lacked a vehicle to coordinate and prioritize their work.

Even before Google developed an interest in book digitization, research libraries had recognized the importance of digitizing their collections. And the dreams of librarians began to shift away from individual library comprehensiveness toward a vision of providing free, open, and public access to all material in digital form. But as with the effort to build a collective collection, libraries found coordination difficult and resources scarce. By 2004, they found themselves with strong third-party interest in their work: an outside technology company in growth mode with seemingly unlimited engineering and financial resources to support their aspirations. When Google stepped into the picture, digitization took off like a rocket.

In this book, we have set out to tell a story about how the vast intellectual heritage of our civilization has become (or will come to be) universally accessible. It is the story of how librarians, scholars, technologists, and entrepreneurs have imagined a global, accessible knowledge source and the extent to which they have succeeded or fallen short in realizing it. This is a story of how digitization has been viewed as the best hope for making our scholarly and cultural heritage universally accessible, and also a story about a sector not yet prepared to leap into the future. It is a story about the limitations of disruptive techno-solutionism in the face of well-coordinated incumbent market leaders, and a story in which some librarians have limited the dream because of financial restrictions and failure of will. It is also a story of the validated knowledge that is still all too absent from an online ecosystem filled with disinformation. And it is a story of how corporate America made the dream palpably real by using computer engineering to productive ends. In this story, there are many actors, all of good intentions. Inevitably, it is also a story of limitations and failures to collaborate. It is a story of how comprehensiveness exists only at a scale greater than any individual organization. Finally, it is a plea to fulfill the dream of making knowledge universally accessible to a world drowning in data and information.

We call this a history of digitization, even though large-scale digitization efforts have been under way for only slightly more than a decade. Digital technology has resulted in such rapid change that libraries and scholarly communication have been transformed in that short period. In viewing the revolutionary decade, we trace the history of library initiatives to digitize and make accessible their legacy collections; we describe the individual efforts to harness digitization for the public good as well as the collaborative efforts to achieve the goal. We look at successes, disappointments, and failures. And throughout, we continue to see possibilities and call on libraries to redouble their efforts to contribute to the massive digital library that can open doors to knowledge for students, scholars, and citizens of the world.

———

In this book, we examine different perspectives on this ideal future. In the first chapter, we trace the history of quests to provide broad access to knowledge and their relative success or failure in fulfilling the dream. We explore the print-based attempts to make scholarly resources more widely available; we follow with those efforts made possible first through automation and later with digital technology.

Chapter 2 goes into detail about the technologists' aspirations for digital technology. Brewster Kahle, researchers at Microsoft, and faculty at Carnegie Mellon University, in particular, had firm notions of societal changes that technology could enable.

Google and its brash rhetoric burst on the scene in chapter 3. Two brilliant computer scientists begin to make the case for a universal digital library. Google was new and not that well known when Sergey Brin and Larry Page first made this argument, and it was frequently met with skepticism. But they had financial resources and they worked fast. Google became a force to be reckoned with.

Chapter 4 deals with the public's expectations for access and how enthusiastically Google's announcement of plans to digitize books was received.

In chapter 5, librarians and scholars begin to organize to respond to the threat or the opportunity of Google. Some of the initiatives were short-lived, but others have had a transformational effect on the nature of scholarship and recorded knowledge.

The lawsuit and the aftermath of the Google settlement are the centerpiece of chapter 6. How did the case develop and why did the proposed settlement fail? More importantly, what opportunities were missed and, now in hindsight, what have been the lasting effects of the Google book digitization initiative?

In chapter 7, we trace some of the efforts to fill the void after the Google project. We examine the possible role HathiTrust may be able to play in building a universal collection.

In the final chapter, we make our own observations about what book digitization in particular and other efforts to provide digital access to scholarly information more broadly have contributed to universal access. Where has there been progress? What else remains?

Finally, in an epilogue, we acknowledge the many changes that emerged in the COVID-19 era, when a greater reliance on technology became a principal strategy for protecting public health, not least in the provision of library services. Though faint, a picture of the future of libraries begins to come into focus.

In addition to capturing an important aspect of scholarly history, we raise a lot of questions about the digital future for the scholarly and information communities. We expect—or at least hope—that university administrators will engage their faculty in discussions about the implications for scholarship, teaching, and the broader public good. And library leaders will renew their efforts to complete the digital agenda that Google started more than a decade ago.

1

Collaborating for Access

The American Library Association was formed in 1876, as part of the Centennial Exposition in Philadelphia. Prominent public librarians, among them Melvil Dewey, met at the Historical Society of Pennsylvania and agreed to form an association with the aim "to enable librarians to do their present work more easily and at less expense."[1] Librarianship was among many other disciplinary specialties that organized itself on this special occasion that marked the centennial of the signing of the Declaration of Independence. Leaders in many fields were invited to attend the exposition to make a statement about the progress the United States had seen in its first century. Over the course of the next century, the library profession in the United States would create a pre-digital network for information sharing and access that was among the greatest the world had ever seen.

1. http://www.ala.org/aboutala/history.

Scholar-Librarians

Librarianship developed into a profession in the decades that would follow, with Melvil Dewey beginning his program of training workers for the public library sector that was burgeoning in part as a result of Andrew Carnegie's philanthropy. Dewey accepted to his library programs classes of majority-female students, helping to forge the profession's identity.[2] But while public librarianship was professionalized in the late nineteenth century, academic research librarianship did not develop into a profession until after World War II. Library directors and bibliographers were generally appointed from the faculty, typically humanists, and most of them continued with their own disciplinary research while managing the library. Catalogers and reference librarians may have been professionally trained, but they provided support services for the faculty who set policy and direction.

It was not until 1932 that the leaders of a group of the largest academic libraries formed the Association of Research Libraries (ARL). And it was not until 1962 that the organization applied to the National Science Foundation for a grant that allowed it to hire a full-time secretariat. Between 1932 and 1962, seven research library directors took turns overseeing the operations of what would grow during this period into a forty-two-member organization. The mission of the original Association of Research Libraries was "by cooperative effort,

---

2. In recent years, Dewey's role has been reassessed in light of claims of sexual harassment and racism. Alison Flood, "Melvil Dewey's Name Stripped from Top Librarian Award," *Guardian*, June 27, 2019, https://www.theguardian.com/books/2019/jun/27/melvil-deweys-name-stripped-from-top-librarian-award.

to develop and increase the resources and usefulness of the research collections in American libraries."[3]

Faculty members who assumed or were assigned responsibility for the campus library used the Association of Research Libraries to pursue large national projects that resulted in more access to scholarly materials for the broad academic community. ARL launched the publication of *Doctoral Dissertations Accepted by American Universities*, which would become *Dissertation Abstracts*. The group created the Committee on Postwar Competition in Book Purchases, which was meant to divide responsibility among its members for ensuring acquisition of materials in more obscure fields. It also funded the publication of *A Catalog of Books Represented by L.C. Printed Cards*, ensuring that scholars would have a resource for finding the libraries holding copies of specific titles.

During the reign of the scholar-librarians, and under the project leadership in many cases of professional librarians, a number of programs were developed that helped researchers gain access to the materials they needed for their work.

Interlibrary Loan

The foundation of the pre-digital network was interlibrary loan. As early as 1886, a librarian at the University of California, Berkeley, U. L. Rowell, developed a plan for interlibrary loan, starting with a partnership with the California State Library. By filling out a form, faculty at UC Berkeley could request delivery of materials held by the state library to their campus.

---

3. Lee Anne George and Julia Blixrud, *Celebrating Seventy Years of the Association of Research Libraries, 1932–2002* (Washington, DC: Association of Research Libraries, 2013).

This system proved to be effective in the early years of implementation, and in the 1890s Rowell invited all of the libraries contributing holdings information to the *National Union Catalog of Manuscript Collections*, maintained by the Library of Congress, to join the interlibrary loan network. The American Library Association (ALA) embraced the notion and created a profession-wide form (ALA Interlibrary Loan Request Form 2002) that all libraries could use to request materials from other libraries in the United States. Relying on the United States Postal Service, participating libraries sent requests to other libraries in the network to borrow materials from their collections. Even though the process was time-intensive, it gave scholars and researchers an opportunity to request materials that would otherwise be unavailable to them.

As time went on, groups of libraries based on size or type or region entered into interlibrary loan agreements that facilitated speedier delivery. In the 1960s, interlibrary loan took on added significance when the Ohio State University Library and others in the state began to create what amounted to a single library system. State funds supported the development of the Ohio College Library Center, a collaborative that presupposed interdependence of libraries in the state, and borrowing materials from one another was a chief benefit. As we will describe in later sections, this "one library" concept, coupled with automation of bibliographic records, gave rise to OCLC, Inc., now a worldwide collaborative that supports thousands of library members.

The Farmington Plan

When Germany invaded Poland in 1939, it was a wake-up call for all research librarians. The great treasures of European libraries upon which so many American scholars depended for their research were threatened with massive destruction. High-level meetings of representatives from the Library of Congress, the American Council of Learned Societies, the Social Science Research Council, the Board on Resources of American Libraries, and the Association of Research Libraries met, beginning in 1939, to develop a plan to ensure access to scholarly resources. The consensus of this group was that library groups and learned societies should develop desiderata of European materials that should be microfilmed by the Library of Congress and made available to the research community. They also concluded that it was essential that the Library of Congress complete the work on building a National Union Catalog so that libraries across the country could locate the research holdings that they might wish to borrow from one another. Wars and natural disasters could easily erase the accumulated knowledge in major research libraries, and American research libraries agreed that they should take responsibility for preservation.

On October 9, 1942, the Executive Committee of the Librarian's Council of the Library of Congress met in Farmington, Connecticut (thus the name of the plan), to discuss next steps.[4] The emerging plan called for a comprehensive collection of currently published materials with individual libraries accepting cooperative responsibility based on subject divisions.[5] The plan was circulated widely within the library community for comment, and it was almost immediately evident that some believed a regional plan was a good idea, while others argued

---

4. For a comprehensive history, see Wagner, *A History of the Farmington Plan.*
5. U.S. Library of Congress, Metcalf-Boyd-MacLeish Committee, *Proposal for a Division of Responsibility among American Libraries in the Acquisition and Recording of Library Materials,* https://crl.acrl.org/index.php/crl/article/view/10049.

for a national approach. Perhaps because the librarians were divided on the best approach the two philanthropic organizations from which the group solicited financial support, the Carnegie Foundation and the Rockefeller Foundation, denied the request. At the Association of Research Libraries' March 1–2, 1944, meeting in New York City, the membership voted to pursue the project on their own and appointed Julian Boyd, Keyes Metcalf, and Archibald MacLeish as a committee to develop a plan.[6]

Among the unique features of the Farmington Plan was the requirement that participating libraries would collect materials in the national interest, even when those materials had negligible interest for the collecting library. A second requirement was that participating libraries would give priority to cataloging the Farmington Plan materials and sending bibliographic information quickly to the Library of Congress for inclusion in the National Union Catalog.

The plan was implemented in 1947, and the Library of Congress *Classification Schedule* was used to assign subject responsibilities to individual libraries across the country. As the plan was self-funded, the committee tried to assign responsibilities based on current collecting strengths of the participating libraries. The plan was restricted to published books, and that, of course, limited the success of the program to collecting only in those countries where book publishing was well established.

The Farmington Plan was a big idea, born out of fear of irreparable loss, but it ultimately failed to serve as the long-term solution for the problem that its leaders had diagnosed. First, it is almost certainly the case that the individual libraries

6. Wagner, *A History of the Farmington Plan*, 94. Minutes of ARL meetings are housed at the offices of the association in Washington, D.C.

that agreed to participate did not prioritize collecting in the assigned subject areas, and they did not have adequate budgets to support the additional responsibilities they had assumed. Second, a federal funding mechanism emerged that supported an alternate national approach. The Agricultural Trade Development and Assistance Act of 1954 (PL 83–480) allowed the United States to sell surplus agricultural products to some forty countries. The countries paid for their purchases with local currencies, or counterpart funds. As a result, the United States developed massive credits that were not needed for military expenditures. Thanks to a remarkable partnership between the American Council of Learned Societies and Congressman John Dingell of Michigan, an amendment to PL 480 was passed that allowed for the purchase of library materials with counterpart funds and authorized the Library of Congress to acquire, index, abstract, and deposit library materials from designated countries. This plan to gather scholarly resources from other parts of the world with federal funds proved to be a far more popular method than a voluntary, self-funded Farmington plan.[7]

The Center for Research Libraries

The aftermath of World War II transformed major research libraries in other ways as well. The GI Bill brought thousands of new students to campuses across the country, and the U.S. government began investing heavily in research and knowledge creation, recognizing that the insular approach of the prewar years could not be repeated. Libraries grew rapidly, and space

7. James E. Skipper, "National Planning for Resource Development" (Association of Research Libraries, 1966), http://www.ideals.uiuc.edu/bitstream/2142/6296/1/librarytrendsv15i2k_opt.pdf.

for collections was a problem. Collections coming from the Farmington Plan or PL 480 had to be retained in the national interest, but they were infrequently used on the local campus. Again, research libraries sought a cooperative solution to the space problems created by building research collections "just in case" they were needed one day. Ten midwestern universities developed a partnership in March 1949 to create the Midwest Inter-Library Corporation (MLC) that allowed participating institutions to send their materials that were little used, but still had research value, to be stored and retrieved when needed from the MLC. The cost was shared based on a formula of the library's acquisitions budget and its university's number of doctoral programs.[8]

In the early 1960s, the MLC became a national organization, the Center for Research Libraries (CRL), under the leadership of Gordon Williams, who launched several national programs in collaboration with the Association of Research Libraries to collect foreign newspapers as part of a permanent, shared collection. CRL also worked with the National Science Foundation to identify and collect international scientific journals for the benefit of the broad scholarly community.

From Scholar to Manager: Change Comes to Research Libraries

Academic librarians pursued broadened access because they worked closely with scholars and researchers. Particularly after World War II, when plentiful research dollars led to an explosion of published literature, scholar-librarians recognized that there was no hope of building local collections that would meet

8. https://www.crl.edu/about/history.

the needs of their faculty and graduate students. While library budgets expanded in the postwar period to provide for better coverage of the research literature, it was clear that no single institution could, on its own, provide the resources needed.

William Dix, legendary university librarian at Princeton in the post–World War II period, in describing leadership qualities of librarians, recognized in this more complicated era of research and publication that the problems of libraries could be solved only by cooperation and collaboration. He called on fellow librarians to concern themselves with the broader community:

> We must concern ourselves with such things as the development of an international cataloging code; new technological advances with potential library applications; the development of libraries and bibliographic tools in other parts of the world. We must engage in research and publication . . . and to inquire and report to the profession the results of these investigations.[9]

Dix recognized that librarians must be contributors to the scholarly ecosystem that included standardizing libraries' bibliographic records so that researchers could more easily locate the resources they were seeking. He understood that the work of professional librarians would grow increasingly important.

The Association of Research Libraries, formed as a club of like-minded scholar-librarians, focused on ways to make more resources available to their faculty members. After World War II,

9. William S. Dix, "Leadership in Academic Libraries," *College and Research Libraries* 21, no. 5 (September 1960): 376.

educational institutions grew quickly. Returning soldiers— older, vocationally focused, part-time students—had different needs than typical college students. New classes, new faculty members, new classrooms were needed, especially on campuses of public institutions. Libraries, by necessity, were required to offer different types of services. University administrators began to recruit library leaders with more managerial experience than scholarly credentials. The ARL added members. It hired its first executive director in 1962. The homogeneous group of library directors could not hold as more of the members were big, public institutions that lived under rules and pressures quite different from those of the private elite institutions.

The new-style library leaders, managers who needed to demonstrate that they could also participate in the scholarly world, were conducting a more practical form of research that indicated growth of library collections was directly linked to the quality of the academic institution. Fremont Rider, college librarian at Wesleyan College and a student of Melvil Dewey, famously calculated that libraries must double in size every fifteen to twenty years in order for their parent institutions to continue to boast high academic ratings.[10] H. William Axford, university librarian of the University of Oregon, tested Rider's research methods in 1962 to determine if Rider's conclusions still held. He examined library statistics from 1946 to 1960 and found that libraries were growing only at 78 percent of the rate Rider had suggested as necessary to maintain academic quality; still, Axford argued that the "relationship between the rate of

10. Fremont Rider, "The Growth of American College and University Libraries— and of Wesleyan's Wesleyan University Library," *About Books* 11 (September 1940): 1–11.

growth of the university library and the over-all quality of the educational program is still essentially correct."[11] Such studies, obviously, exerted pressure on university and college administrators to spend more on library acquisitions. The large, elite institutions competed with one another to assemble massive research libraries in the post–World War II era, but not all institutions could invest as much, and some administrators began to question the necessity of doing so.

Robert Munn, while serving as the acting provost and dean of the graduate school at West Virginia University, coined the term "bottomless pit" to describe the academic library: "many administrators view the library as a bottomless pit. They have observed that increased appropriations one year invariably result in still larger requests the next. More important, there do not appear to be even any theoretical limits to the library's needs."[12] This attitude was indicative of the shift from seeing the library as a scholarly resource to an example of administrative overhead. Academic librarians could ill afford to have university administrators thinking of them in this way, and it has yielded a steady shift toward taking a more managerial approach to library collections and services, including greater investment in a variety of schemes for sharing resources that would offer many options for faculty and students and sometimes the general public to gain access to institutions' collections, without adding excessively to the local budgets.

11. H. William Axford, "Rider Revisited," *College and Research Libraries* 23 (1962): 345–47.

12. Robert F. Munn, "The Bottomless Pit, or, The Academic Library as Viewed from the Administration Building," *College and Research Libraries* 29, no. 1 (January 1968): 52.

Centralized Document Delivery

By the late 1960s, the U.S. government had taken an interest in providing broad access to information. President Lyndon Johnson's Great Society in the 1960s included a consideration of the role libraries could play in supporting the needs of society. He created a national commission on libraries to "make a comprehensive study and appraisal of the role of libraries as resources for scholarly pursuits, as centers for the dissemination of knowledge and as components of the evolving information systems." The commission recommended the establishment of a permanent, independent agency that would act as the federal planning agency for library policy. In 1970, the National Commission on Library and Information Science (NCLIS) was created to take on the responsibility.

This development caught the attention of publishers. Throughout the post–World War II twentieth century, librarians struggled with the explosion of publishing and sought collaborative ways to rationalize collections and manage cost, but during the same period, publishers were enjoying the expanding sales to libraries as they built ever larger collections. Publishers wondered if government policy might promote collaboration among libraries, thereby reducing the overall purchases from publishers.

In the United Kingdom, government programs emerged as the most effective method of rationalizing library resources. Because the government coordinated the services and funding for research libraries came from a central source, such a service could be managed without having to work through consensus. In the early 1970s, the British Library was established as an independent government agency, and it assumed responsibility for the British Library Document Supply Service housed in the

Boston Spa facility. The service was built on a central collection of periodicals housed in Yorkshire that could be made available to any of the higher education institutions of the United Kingdom, as well as to the general public.

The library community in the United States believed that such a service would be important for the United States as well and prevailed upon the new NCLIS to undertake a feasibility study for such a service. The NCLIS staff, being quite small, felt ill-equipped to conduct the study and asked the Library of Congress to lead it. The Library of Congress did not have research staff to devote to the effort and commissioned the Council on Library Resources (CLR) to carry out the study. Just as the study was being launched, Warren J. Haas, university librarian at Columbia, was appointed president of CLR. Haas had a firm knowledge of this interest in developing a national coordinated service of periodicals, what was soon to become known as the National Periodicals Center (NPC). He had served on CLR's board during the discussions of the need for the NPC, and he was one of its most ardent supporters. Haas immediately raised the necessary funds to carry out the study, and in 1978, the Council on Library Resources published *A National Periodicals Center Technical Development Plan*.[13]

The sole purpose of the NPC would be to create a centralized repository that could respond rapidly to requests for individual articles. The bibliographic information about the journals and their contents would reside in a national database and the NPC would be governed by a board made up of national leaders who would establish policy and oversee operations. The creators of

13. For a fuller history, see Mary Biggs, "The Proposed National Periodicals Center, 1973–1980: Study, Dissension, and Retreat," *Resource Sharing & Information Networks* 1, issue 3–4 (1984), https://doi.org/10.1300/J121v01n03_01.

the plan recognized that the potential of emerging automation would be essential to its implementation. The publishing and information management communities exploded in opposition to any plan that made library resources more readily available to the public without compensating publishers. The National Commission on Libraries and Information Science held congressional hearings on the proposed NPC, and the death knell of the plan was sounded when Representative William Ford (D-MI) commented on the confusion, "We can't tell where you people (the library community) stand." The library community was deeply divided among those who wanted national programs to lead very large and complicated services, and those who wanted regional or local initiatives to have priority. Ultimately, weak enabling legislation was passed to authorize a National Periodicals Center, but funding was never appropriated for the purpose.[14] Efforts to create the National Periodicals Center and their eventual failure vividly illustrate the challenges that the library community in the United States has had in establishing centralized vehicles to enable collaboration.

Automation and the Role of Standards

Since Melvil Dewey's professionalization of librarianship, the cataloging record for items in the collection has been at the core. Collaboration among libraries has been possible because all (or most) of them used the same conventions for describing their collections. As a result, visitors to any library in the country could readily discern the collections available for local use or for sharing through interlibrary loan.

---

14. Martin C. Cummings, ed., *Influencing Change in Research Librarianship: A Festschrift for Warren J. Haas* (Washington, DC: Council on Library Resources, 1988), 22.

Prior to an automated system for capturing bibliographic information, the Library of Congress, and nearly all other libraries, used hand-produced catalog cards that were filed according to library rules in drawers we remember from childhood. Prior to automated processes, libraries around the country created their own catalog cards to describe their local collections. Participating libraries made one extra copy of the catalog records they produced and sent them to the Library of Congress (LC). At regular intervals, LC filed all of these cards in alphabetical order by author and made photocopied pages of these cards and published books of the records. The Library of Congress began producing the *National Union Catalog of Pre-1956 Imprints* in the 1950s. It was published by Mansell as a set of 754 volumes and largely superseded the older *Library of Congress Catalog of Printed Books*, and included printed works published before 1956 that are held by major American and Canadian libraries. Libraries purchased these sets and added them to their reference collections for their patrons to consult when looking for works not housed in their local libraries. These books of catalog cards formed the basis for interlibrary loan of scholarly resources.

Collaboration among libraries became much easier when automation pioneer Henriette Avram introduced Machine Readable Cataloging (MARC) at the Library of Congress in the 1960s. MARC is a computerized method of recording the information elements of a cataloging record: the descriptive cataloging, subject headings and other access points, and classification numbers and other call number information. Creating these computer-readable cataloging records meant that computer programs could be designed to search for and display specified pieces of the information stored in a cataloging record. Avram came from the National Security Agency, and although she had to educate herself in the arcane practices of librarianship, she understood very well that information could be shared far more effectively if it could be read by computers. The conversion of miles of catalog card drawers in the nation's largest library took seven years. Libraries across the nation watched the process with great interest, because up until that time they had only a primitive method of sharing the contents of their libraries with others.

After the Library of Congress adopted MARC as its standard, the next logical step was to convert its card catalogs to an automated format that could be easily shared with other institutions. The conversion project would be huge, the library realized, but it would be a major step toward creating a network of libraries that allowed for massive resource sharing. As the most trusted source for bibliographic data, the Library of Congress remained the authoritative source of bibliographic information and, through the 1980s at least, the authoritative source of information about what materials were housed at other libraries.

The Library of Congress did not act unilaterally. Working closely with other English-speaking national libraries, a group of cataloging experts worked for years on a unified cataloging code, recognizing that technology was going to make sharing bibliographic information ever easier; but without common cataloging rules, it would be impossible to share catalog records with users in a meaningful way. In 1976, the English-speaking national libraries' joint effort to establish common cataloging rules was issued in the form of *Anglo-American Cataloging Rules*.[15] The effort to use common rules for bibliographic

---

15. American Library Association, *Anglo-American Cataloging Rules* (Chicago: American Library Association, 1976).

description disrupted the library world. The Library of Congress's implementation of the rules affected every library that relied on the same database of bibliographic records. When the Library of Congress began to sell its cataloging records to libraries around the globe, those records were most useful when the local libraries adopted the Library of Congress's bibliographic rules.

When the Anglo-American national libraries reached an agreement that all of them would adopt the new cataloging rules by 1980, they were confronted with a major decision with profound financial implications. Would they "freeze" their card catalogs and begin using automated systems for all bibliographic records after 1976? Or would they try to continue to maintain massive numbers of catalog cards, making necessary changes to bring all of the records into conformance with the new code?

The Library of Congress announced that it would close its card catalog with 1976 imprints. Other research libraries, with smaller numbers of records to process, converted their catalog cards to digital files that could be entered into their online catalogs and shared easily with users much sooner. The 1970s was one of the library community's most stressful transformations. The Association of Research Libraries, after the development of the MARC standard, created a committee to study the future of card catalogs.[16] The ability to render bibliographic information in machine-readable form had enormous implications for sharing and reusing bibliographic records, but the benefits would be realized only if a great number of libraries made the mental

---

16. Association of Research Libraries, *The Future of Card Catalogs* (Washington, DC: Association of Research Libraries, 1975).

transition from stand-alone institutions with locally developed rules for bibliographic control to nodes in a national network.

Many of these library practices would have seemed arcane to the scholarly community, but they were necessary to build a network of scholarly communication in which individual libraries served as nodes in a national network that allowed for unimpeded information flow. Much of the credit for developing the national nodes concept goes to the OCLC and its founder, Frederick Kilgour. Presidents of Ohio universities and colleges wanted to develop a computerized library network that would make it possible for their institutions to share cataloging information easily in order to save money. The group of presidents and library directors met at Ohio State University in 1967 to form a nonprofit organization to be called the Ohio College Library Center and they hired Kilgour, former medical librarian at Yale University, as a consultant to develop a plan for them. Kilgour created a computer network that linked libraries in Ohio to a centralized database, making it possible for one library to reuse the cataloging records that had been created by another. The growth of the Ohio College Library Center coincided with the creation of a new international cataloging code and with the growing interest on the part of libraries across the nation to move from manual, local systems to network-based automated systems. By 1978, the Ohio College Library Center was well-enough established to drop "Ohio" from its name to become a national organization, known simply as OCLC, Inc., and offer membership to libraries everywhere. While it was established as a catalog-sharing resource, it was immediately clear that thinking about libraries as nodes of a network offered a new vision for the future of these organizations, and technology was emerging quickly to make new dreams possible.

This process of "automating" library catalogs drove meaningful cost efficiencies in cataloging. It made the processing of interlibrary loan requests far faster and more efficient, which in turn allowed a library to take into account others' collections in considering one's local acquisitions. And it led to improvements in discovery, since first librarians and then end users could search the collections of other catalogs and OCLC's online catalog (which came to be called WorldCat) to see what was available across the collective collection of all libraries. These opportunities arose from nothing more than the digital availability of what we today call the metadata about our collections. No digitization of the underlying content had yet been undertaken, but the stage was set for thinking of libraries as a national network of information resources.

Bibliographic Systems

While digital technology brought disruptive change to libraries, it was not entirely new. Mainframe computers and their ability to process and disseminate large amounts of data became commonplace in large research libraries in the 1970s. The Library of Congress's Avram recognized that manually reproducing cards could not be sustained; by automating the cataloging process, bibliographic data could be shared and repurposed. By creating the MARC code in a public institution, the cataloging records of the Library of Congress were captured on magnetic tape and could easily be distributed to other libraries that wanted to use the MARC records for their own purposes. The era of bibliographic systems quickly emerged.

While the advantages of automation were apparent, it was equally clear that few academic libraries would be positioned to take advantage of it with existing resources and approaches.

Library directors had to look beyond their organizations to recruit computer scientists who could develop the systems to make productive use of the new tools. At the same time, many academic computer scientists were looking for applications for the computing power they had recently acquired. The library proved to be a great partner.

A few of the largest research libraries took an entrepreneurial approach and built their own library systems, purchasing MARC tapes from the Library of Congress to begin populating them. Pioneering mainframe-based systems such as Stanford's BALLOTS (Bibliographic Automation of Large Library Operations), the University of Chicago's Integrated Library System, Washington Library Network's acquisitions and cataloging network, and Northwestern University Library's NOTIS (Northwestern On-Line Total Integrated System) project were developed to solve local bibliographic problems. Several were soon commercialized, which meant that the development and maintenance costs could be shared across multiple organizations and thereby enabling far more libraries to adopt these systems than if local development were required.

The Council on Library Resources, under the leadership of Warren J. Haas, did not want to cede development of automated library systems to the commercial world. With $6 million in funding from multiple foundations and the National Endowment for the Humanities, Haas created the Bibliographic Services Development Program. The aim of the program was to explore the technical and political aspects of networking necessary to bring a nationwide bibliographic service into existence. The program built on the already underway efforts of the Library of Congress and the emerging bibliographic utilities and regional library networks. The role of the Council on Library Resources was to find a way to link all of these systems to each other. Haas understood that developing a national bibliographic system required collaboration among library systems, as well as support from the broader scholarly community. The CLR created a membership committee charged with overseeing the program.[17] The work of the Bibliographic Services Development Program (BSDP) was completed when the CLR brokered an agreement among the networks such that any library record that was contributed to one of the national bibliographic utilities (OCLC or Research Libraries Group) would be automatically copied to the other.

These initiatives in the 1970s and early 1980s, grounded in the logic of the mainframe computer, focused on sharing the development of local platforms and through them catalog records so that librarians could inform their users of the locations of books and articles they were interested in. Since so many networks were created during this period, the greatest concern was that scholars would be confused by the multitudes of resources. In little more than a single decade, the ability to share information via digital technology made the BSDP efforts seem primitive. With digital technology, the information itself, not simply the bibliographic description of the information, could be easily and quickly shared.

17. The committee included the chief executive officers of the three major bibliographic networks: Frederic Kilgour of OCLC, Inc., Edward Shaw of the Research Libraries Group, and Roderick Swartz of the Washington Library Network, along with Herman Fussler of the Graduate Library School of the University of Chicago, Henriette Avram of the Library of Congress, and Carol Ishimoto of Harvard University. A management committee, made up of Frederick Burkhardt, past president of the American Council of Learned Societies and first chairman of the National Commission on Libraries and Information Science, William Welsh, Deputy Librarian of Congress, and CLR president Warren J. Haas of the Council on Library Resources, guided the work. Association of Research Libraries, *Newsletter*, no. 95 (February 26, 1979): 4.

Structures for Collaboration

Sustained attention to various types of work to make collections more accessible shows the extent to which improving discovery and access has been a universal value and goal for the library field. As academia grew in the late nineteenth century, scholar-librarians banded together to ensure that their colleagues would have access to the materials needed to conduct their research. And as academia mushroomed after 1945, these scholar-librarians and the more professionalized library leadership to whom they eventually gave way sought mechanisms to guarantee access to priority collections and to reduce their collective expenditure in doing so. With interlibrary loan as the foundation, they created one of the most successful pre-digital networks for information sharing and access, with the vast majority of the network self-organized. And they managed to transition it successfully to digital form, with the automation and standardization of library catalogs and cataloging practices.

While there were many successes in the creation of this self-organized system, there was also evidence of structural limitations. Whereas the successful national-level collaborations provided strong incentives for a given library to opt in, efforts like Farmington that required aligned local investments on a sustained basis or those like the National Periodicals Center that required libraries to coordinate their efforts by speaking with a single voice were not to succeed. To be successful, it seems that a collaboration had to leverage the self-organizing preferences or abilities of the network participants rather than attempt to centralize them in some way.

Even with all of the success in creating this information-sharing and access network, the efforts of libraries to make their collections more broadly accessible were largely focused on enabling discovery that would allow the physical movement of print materials. Librarians took pride in their ability to locate books and journals across the country for their local users. The next logical step for libraries, with this foundation of collaboration, was to harness digital technology to convert collections to electronic form so that they could easily be shared immediately with anyone, anywhere. Libraries' wariness of commercial enterprises was a difficult barrier to overcome, and many collaborative organizations grew out of a desire to make progress inside the circle of trusted partners rather than going outside it.

2

The Dreamers

When librarians built collections of books and journals, the decisions were their own, with input from scholars who had a strong interest in the library's contents. Digital technology resulted in introducing other players into the library's governance and processes. In his *Forbes* article of 2015, Gil Press[1] traces the history of digitization from 1679 when Gottfried Wilhelm Leibniz developed the modern binary number system to 2015 when the McKinsey Global Institute published "Digital America: A Tale of the Haves and Have-Mores," the first major attempt to measure the ongoing digitization of the U.S. economy at a sector level.[2] His short history makes clear

1. Gil Press, "A Very Short History of Digitization," *Forbes*, December 27, 2015, https://www.forbes.com/sites/gilpress/2015/12/27/a-very-short-history-of-digitization/#53f554a649ac.

2. McKinsey Global Institute, "Digital America: A Tale of the Haves and Have-Mores," December 1, 2015, https://www.mckinsey.com/industries/technology-media-and-telecommunications/our-insights/digital-america-a-tale-of-the-haves-and-have-mores.

that the advent of digital technology transformed knowledge production and dissemination as well as the broader American economy. Technological visionaries could easily imagine that this technology could be harnessed for a broad public purpose. With declining costs of scanning, the widespread availability of computers, and most importantly the inception of the Internet, all recorded knowledge could be digitized and made accessible. It was a simple matter of using the technology that was now available.

Advocating a Digital Vision

Digital technology gave rise to wide-ranging possibilities for solving some of society's pressing problems. Vice President Al Gore, addressing the International Telecommunications Union in 1994, imagined the universal digital library. Latching on to the political possibilities for technology to give greater opportunity for all, he opined, "The Global Information Infrastructure will help educate our children and allow us to exchange ideas within a community and among nations. It will be a means by which families and friends will transcend the barriers of time and distance. It will make possible a global information marketplace, where consumers can buy or sell products."[3] In academic and library communities, Vice President Gore's rallying cry would translate to a mandate for rendering massive print collections into ones and zeros so that libraries could achieve their ultimate dream: to make their collections available to everyone, everywhere. Scholars and students were not

---

3. Vice President Al Gore, Information Superhighways Speech, International Telecommunications Union, March 21, 1994, http://vlib.iue.it/history/internet/algorespeech.html.

necessarily as concerned about the ways in which library collections could be shared. From their perspective digitization meant that they would be able to find and use information from a wide variety of sources: libraries, publishers, other scholars, and other organizations—all from the convenience of their own computer.

Libraries' efforts to develop their collaborations around cataloging, resource sharing, and automation, such as those we saw in chapter 1, were thus met with new opportunities, and also competition, from the advances in digital technology. Realizing the potential of converting text itself to a machine-readable format, several individuals and organizations immediately accepted the benefits of digitization and began dreaming of how the new technology could lead to a utopian future of everyone, everywhere having access to the world's knowledge.

Some of the dreamers came from the private sector and thought about the possibilities of digitization on a grander scale. Digital technology sparked enthusiasm among computer scientists and others for creating new resources for the public good, unlocking digitizing library collections and making these materials freely available to all. Computer scientists had none of the connections to the world of bibliography and cataloging. For them, the technology that allowed books to be converted to digital form had the advantage of easily sharing content with anyone who had access to a computer. Books did not have to be stored on shelves in libraries. They did not have to be cataloged for retrieval. They did not need to be grouped together by subject. Technology allowed simple word searching, freeing book content from the principles and practices of library science, so its advocates had little understanding of how libraries had been organized traditionally nor did they feel any particular need to acquire it. For them, book digitization offered a compelling case study in the power of computing. For them, the challenge, if they recognized it, was to find librarians who shared their vision and would agree to work with them.

In other cases, library leaders saw for themselves the opportunity. Many of these leaders were a new breed of librarian, ones who had been brought into research libraries and in some cases into the library profession as a result of the need to develop and maintain the bibliographic systems discussed in chapter 1. These leaders saw opportunities to marry digital technologies including the emerging Internet with the research and learning needs of their users and the management requirements of their libraries. Their challenge was typically that they were constrained by their organizational perspective from recognizing the transformational, and in some cases disruptive, potential that accompanied the vision they were pursuing.

Gloriana St. Clair and Raj Reddy

Among the earliest projects to digitize books was the Million Book Project, hosted at Carnegie Mellon University (CMU). Computer scientist Raj Reddy, professor at Carnegie Mellon, and Gloriana St. Clair, the CMU library director, formed a promising partnership to explore the possibilities of digital technology and announced the Million Book Digital Library[4] project in 2000. The objective was to create a "free-to-read, searchable collection of one million books, primarily in the English language, available to everyone over the Internet."[5] Reddy and St. Clair observed that the typical large high school library generally held fewer than 30,000 volumes. The Million

---

4. Not to be confused with Million Book Project, an effort to make books available to incarcerated individuals. https://millionbookproject.org/.

5. http://www.rr.cs.edu/mbdl.htm.

Book library would be the equivalent of a substantial university library, and it would be easily and freely accessible to everyone in the world.

They set out to digitize books in current libraries, focusing on pre-1920 materials in the public domain. They began by identifying titles in a premier reference source, *Books for College Libraries*. After as many of those books as possible had been identified and scanned, they planned to recruit scholars in different disciplines to select additional titles of importance to be added to their digital library. Reddy and St. Clair secured a grant of $500,000 from the National Science Foundation (NSF) to cover the cost of equipment—scanners, computers, servers, and software. They planned to recruit American research libraries to identify titles they would ship to China and India, where the scanning would be done at a modest cost before being returned to the library of origin. Reaching the million-book goal was to be accomplished before 2005.

The result would be a large-scale library open 24 hours a day, 7 days a week, 365 days a year. Many readers could use the materials simultaneously—books would never be "checked out" to other readers. All people, in remote locations in the United States and everywhere else in the world, would have unfettered access to educational resources.

Reddy also hoped for another result: an extensive test bed for textual language processing research. He wanted to include at least 10,000 of the million books available in more than one language used as a test for problems in example-based machine translation.

The project leaders sought help from members of the Digital Library Federation, of which Carnegie Mellon was a participant. To demonstrate the efficacy of the project before they sought NSF funding, CMU librarians began with a pilot to digitize 100 books. Two problems were immediately evident.

In order to scan books rapidly, the books had to be disbound and fed automatically through the scanner. The "guillotine" that was used to separate the books' pages from their bindings cost $10,000, a hefty layout for the CMU libraries. They also discovered that the dust that had accumulated on older books caused frequent jamming of the scanner, and the librarians had to clean the equipment often to keep it running. The pilot made it clear that they had to find another way to accomplish the task.

In a subsequent 1,000-book project, CMU abandoned the inexpensive duplex scanners and the guillotining of books. The library bought a much more expensive overhead scanner that allowed books to be scanned without removing the bindings and adjusted for curvature and different paper thickness and texture—and tolerated book dust.

Reddy and St. Clair found willing partners in Chinese and Indian universities but never succeeded in convincing U.S. libraries to contribute to the project. Even so, by December 2007, they had scanned 1.5 million books in 20 languages and established partial mirror sites in India, China, the Internet Archive, Bibliotheca Alexandrina, and Carnegie Mellon University. The NSF invested just under $4 million in equipment and administrative travel for the project. The government of India invested $25 million to support language translation research projects, and the Ministry of Education in China contributed $8.5 million over three years to the project. Yet, without a strong participation by U.S. libraries, the Million Book Project became a proof of concept for the Google Book Search and the Internet Archive book-scanning projects rather than a digital library.

A possible reason for negligible take-up of the Million Book Project is that librarians had mixed feelings about the advances being made by the computer scientists. It seemed to librarians that computer scientists were more focused on demonstrating that a digital library could be assembled. While the computer scientists seemed content with gathering up any million books they could find, librarians noted that they had been collecting and preserving books at the title level for centuries. Computer scientists were proposing initiatives that would make the contents of those books widely and easily accessible to a worldwide audience, but librarians wondered if this should not be the work of libraries themselves. They understood that scholars' use of the resource would depend upon the quality, value, and demand for the books in the collection. For at least a few library directors, there was a desire to lead such transformational efforts rather than collaborate with the Carnegie Mellon initiative. Funding possibilities seemed certain for the libraries that could innovate with digital technology. It also provided an opportunity to demonstrate to university administrators that the library was in the technological vanguard. It would have been difficult to achieve the same kind of recognition by collaborating with other institutions.

While library directors considered how to make the best use of digital technology on their own campuses, a few individuals deserve special attention, for they took it upon themselves to move ahead with demonstrating the societal benefits of digital collections. Their leadership, though sometimes controversial, clearly paved the way for all libraries to confront their digital futures.

Brewster Kahle and the Internet Archive

After graduating from MIT in 1982 with a bachelor's degree in computer science and engineering, Brewster Kahle worked in companies focused on artificial intelligence. At Thinking

Machines, he and other colleagues developed the WAIS system, a precursor of the World Wide Web. Two companies developed by Kahle, WAIS, Inc., and Alexa Internet, were subsequently sold to AOL and Amazon, respectively, and Kahle used the substantial proceeds to fund the Internet Archive. The mission of his new organization was to collect and index everything on the World Wide Web. As a gatherer of information, Kahle thought of himself as a librarian, even giving himself the title of "founder and digital librarian." He saw his work as equivalent to that of print-based librarians who had carefully gathered recorded knowledge. He thought it would be easy to recruit librarians to join his efforts to gather the rapidly growing body of digital resources. But Kahle, a man of action, also grew impatient with all of the conversations that librarians were having among themselves. He did not see any reason to be so deliberative. His interest was in developing a comprehensive digital library, not talking about the relative merits of the traditional versus digital library that seemed to dominate the discussions of academic librarians.

Kahle found more inspiration from fellow computer scientists. He had taken notice of the power of digitization when he was introduced to Michael Hart's work on Project Gutenberg, calling him someone who understood the power of universal access. Kahle followed the work of computer scientists Raj Reddy at Carnegie Mellon and Michael Lesk at the National Science Foundation, and he began working on establishing scanning centers that used custom-designed scanners and engineering methods that resulted in low-cost, high-quality digital scans. Kahle was equally impatient with a copyright law that was written for the print environment. He did not want to openly defy the law, however, so he took the position that the law allowed reformatting of in-copyright works to make them available to blind and physically handicapped persons. That would be the defense for scanning books, not fair use.

In 1996, when Kahle used funding from his for-profit web-crawling venture, Alexa Internet, to create the not-for-profit Internet Archive to crawl and preserve websites, he created the "Internet Library" that would be freely available to the public. From the beginning, Kahle emphasized the power of technology to unlock information stores. Digital technology allowed everyone to have access to the resources libraries had been able to make available only locally. Kahle was exuberantly enthusiastic about technology's promise and downplayed the concerns raised by traditional librarians.

While building a large cache of websites that the Internet Archive would preserve, Kahle also invested Internet Archive funds to create scanning centers, and he began contacting libraries to interest them in joining his initiative to build a digital library. He hoped that libraries would agree to have their collections scanned at his centers, contributing to the development of a massive digital resource that would be freely available to all. In 2004, Kahle received the Paul Evan Peters Award, jointly granted from the Association of Research Libraries, the Coalition for Networked Information (CNI), and EDUCAUSE, in recognition of the most notable and lasting international achievements related to information technology and the creation and use of information resources and services that advance scholarship and intellectual productivity. In his acceptance speech at the CNI conference and later at the spring meeting of the Association of Research Libraries, Kahle described his plans for scanning centers and asked library directors this question: If he could scan the materials in their libraries at ten cents a page, would they be willing to send their books to be digitized? Most of the directors simply chose not to respond, although at least three—Donald Waters from the Andrew W. Mellon Foundation, Winston Tabb from the Library of Congress, and Carole Moore of the University of Toronto—asked for more information. Only Carole Moore, according to Kahle, followed through with a plan for digitizing the collections of the University of Toronto Libraries.[6] With the digitization labs established and industrial processes in place to keep costs very low, Kahle was deeply disappointed by the response from the library community.

When Kahle had first become aware of Google's plan to digitize books—about which we will see much more in chapter 3—he had approached the company about forming some type of partnership, but he had been rebuffed. He hoped librarians would be more receptive to his plans. Knowing that other technology companies had their own misgivings about Google, he went next to Yahoo!, Microsoft, the University of Toronto, and the University of California to gain support for establishing the Open Content Alliance to offer an alternative approach to book digitization. Instead of following an opt-out policy, the Open Content Alliance secured the copyright holder's permission and then scanned and stored book content at the Internet Archive for freely available distribution. Kahle ardently pursued philanthropic and library support for the consortial effort as a counter to the privatization of knowledge that he feared from Google.

Kahle's vision for the universal library eventually expanded to include not only digitized books but also videos, films, audio recordings, games, and television broadcasts. With each new format, copyright and intellectual property questions arose, but while maintaining an opt-out policy for knowledge creators,

6. Deanna Marcum, interview with Brewster Kahle, February 16, 2016.

Kahle was able to proceed without encountering serious legal barriers (his approach to copyright would eventually change). He invited librarians to join his crusade for freely open and universal digital libraries, and he established a number of digitization centers and hired staff to carry out the work as a way to entice libraries to contribute content to the Internet Archive.

James H. Billington and the Library of Congress

Digital technology also fueled the dreams of the Librarian of Congress. The Library of Congress (LC) was among the first library organizations to think about using digital technology to expand its mission. Librarian James Billington was appointed by President Ronald Reagan in 1987. A Princeton-educated Harvard professor and the long-time head of the Woodrow Wilson International Center for Scholars, Billington, at his swearing-in ceremony, pledged to "get the champagne out of the bottle," using technology to make the rich collections of the Nation's Library available to a much broader audience. He believed that exposing students to the foundational historical documents would prompt them to ask questions, to dig more deeply into their own history.

He created the American Memory project in 1990 before the Internet was widely deployed and relied on CD-ROM technology as a primary distribution mechanism for the digitized primary source documents relating to American history. The digitized collections were stored on CD-ROMs that were distributed to forty-four schools and libraries. The lessons from the CD-ROM pilot were encouraging: students and their teachers were making good use of these digitized materials. They were excited about having access to primary source materials. The harder lesson was that using CD-ROM technology was both difficult and exorbitantly expensive. In 1992, Billington recruited Laura Campbell, who had a background in accounting and strategic planning and had been working in a consulting firm, to lead the American Memory project. Campbell was charged by Billington with finding a better way to distribute the library's content to the public.

The Internet came along at a perfect time. By 1994, the Library of Congress was ready to give up on its experiment with CD-ROMs, but by thinking creatively about how to move from the inadequate technology of CD-ROMs to the newest innovation, the Internet, the library convinced a number of organizations and individuals to help. Congress agreed to provide $5 million to start scanning collections, with the promise that if the library could demonstrate success, more money would follow. The library solicited a donation from David Packard, the cofounder of Hewlett Packard, who was especially eager to help get information out of the library and into the hands of students and researchers. John E. Kluge, the chairman of Metromedia, gave $5 million, and the W. K. Kellogg Foundation contributed $3 million. The $13 million in donations gave the Library of Congress such a jump start that it reached its goal of raising $45 million for the project from the private sector, and Congress added another $15 million.

Members of Congress, especially Speaker of the House Newt Gingrich, loved the plan. Congressional representatives could easily see that making the riches of the Nation's Library available to their constituents would be a popular program. The development of the Internet and the World Wide Web encouraged loose talk about making the contents of the Library of Congress freely available to all.

The library's program was warmly embraced by both the House and the Senate. Speaker Gingrich agreed that federal dollars would match the private gift of Kluge, and Senator Ted Stevens, a long-time friend of Billington, spearheaded a bill that was passed in December 2000 that promised $100 million to the Library of Congress to digitize and digitally preserve its collections. The focus went beyond the Library of Congress to include working with other federal agencies and other stakeholders to agree on a national approach to preserving the digital collections as they were created.

Billington admired Campbell's business acumen and her ability to get things done. Not from the library world, she was more focused on how to make collections available to the public than on cataloging practices or policies about scanning entire collections instead of selected items from the collection. With the money he had raised from Congress and the private sector, Billington was confident enough to set a goal of scanning five million items by 2001, at the end of the library's bicentennial year. He needed someone who could manage very large, technical projects and deliver on deadline.

Campbell had been working in the Library of Congress long enough as a consultant to know that the bureaucracy did not nurture start-up technological projects easily. With private funding in hand, she hired a cadre of young, technically capable college graduates to build the American Memory team. They worked with subject specialists and collections curators to identify the most historically significant primary source materials and began to scan them. Most of the materials were housed in special collections divisions and had not been cataloged. Tagging and retrieval became difficult issues without accompanying cataloging information, but the goal of five million items by the year 2001 required the team to improvise. They identified collections and scanned materials into collection folders. Although more a museum approach than a library approach, it worked, at least in the early days of American Memory. The federal effort excited librarians around the country, and many research libraries laid out plans to digitize and make accessible their collections, though nearly all planned to do so with the funds they secured from private foundations.

The Library of Congress, facing increased criticism from the library community for not doing more to collaborate, responded by securing a $2 million grant from Ameritech to incorporate digital materials from other libraries into American Memory. It started with material from the New-York Historical Society (which provided its Civil War collection) and the Chicago Historical Society (the holder of the archives of the *Chicago Daily News*, a defunct newspaper with a notable sports collection). Later, competitive grants were offered to smaller libraries and historical societies to allow them to digitize their unique materials to be added to American Memory.

The Library of Congress made a fundamental decision to avoid scanning its book collections, largely because the leadership believed that the books could be found in a variety of libraries, but the special collections materials were unique and could be used to stimulate imagination and learning in the education community. It would similarly take a focused approach to engage in the Google book digitization project, as we discuss in chapter 3.

Wendy Lougee and the University of Michigan

Paul Courant, economist and provost at the University of Michigan, was relatively new in his position when he was introduced to Larry Page of Google, but he had been vice provost for budget for the previous five years, so he was keenly aware of the financial pressures libraries placed on their universities through his conversations with library director William Gosling. In his words, he was "seduced by the vision of the universal digital library. I wanted free, open access to everything, always. It was clear to me that technology makes that vision economically and technically easy. It was already clear to me that this was the direction we should be taking in the academy. The digital revolution was the right direction, but we were digitizing about ten thousand works a year."[7] For the economist, digital copies of library holdings offered huge advantages for preservation and for information retrieval, but the staff capacity to use the technology for these purposes was limited.

The University of Michigan had been taking important steps toward a digital library—small in retrospect but nationally groundbreaking at the time. Wendy Pradt Lougee had been hired as the head of the Harlan Hatcher Graduate Library and had the opportunity to reimagine collection development, reference, and access services at the university. Lougee hired a cadre of subject specialists who were given responsibility for outreach to departments served by the Graduate Library. As Lougee and her colleagues wrote in chronicling the development of the digital library, "Almost unnoticed in this transformation of core services was a small cadre of younger librarians that Wendy recruited and supported, who, among other more traditional responsibilities, were interested in expanding the range and distribution of electronic resources in the humanities and social sciences. These librarians worked with Lougee's support to extend electronic access to government information and, later, to literary texts."[8]

7. Deanna Marcum, interview with Paul Courant, May 25, 2016.

8. Maria Bonn, Patricia Hodges, Mark Sandler, and John Wilkin, "Building the Digital Library at the University of Michigan," in Patricia Hodges, Maria Bonn, Mark

The electronic resources group at Michigan was years ahead of federal government agencies in considering how to disseminate information in digital form, so they took matters into their own hands. They began to acquire text files and encode them with SGML tags. Lougee supported this work by negotiating the appropriate software licenses that allowed the young "geeks," as they described themselves, to acquire the digital files that they could turn into distributable scholarly resources. Lougee realized that gaining access to these resources required a different kind of organizational structure that went beyond typical library acquisitions. She encouraged her staff in developing Michigan's first text-analysis system called UMLibText and made it available to faculty and students. Even though it was a primitive system, other librarians on the staff and administrators began to take notice.

Publishers were also taking notice of the transformational capabilities of digital technology. Library leaders in a number of universities had approached Elsevier to see if there might be some way to accelerate the development of large-scale systems for the distribution of journals in electronic form. Elsevier had been considering the same question from the publisher's perspective and was looking for experience on which to make informed strategic decisions. Elsevier and nine university libraries collaborated to develop a project, known as TULIP (The University Licensing Program), to determine the feasibility of the networked distribution of journals, to understand the economic and practical viability of the method, and to study

Sandler, and John Price Wilkin, *Digital Libraries: A Vision for the 21st Century: A Festschrift in Honor of Wendy Lougee on the Occasion of Her Departure from the University of Michigan* (Ann Arbor: Michigan Publishing, University of Michigan Library, 2003), http://dx.doi.org/10.3998/spobooks.bbv9812.0001.001.

usage patterns. The University of Michigan was one of the participating institutions.[9]

In 1995, university librarian Gosling traded on the national reputation the University of Michigan had attained as a creator and distributor of electronic resources to secure funds from the Andrew W. Mellon Foundation to enter into a digitization project with Cornell University called Making of America (MOA) in 1995. By this time Lougee had been named associate director of the University Library for Digital Library Services and had a national reputation for imagining how digitization could transform libraries. She, along with colleagues at Cornell University Libraries, had been disappointed that the Library of Congress announced its American Memory initiative without partnering with major research libraries. Lougee and Anne Kenney of Cornell set out to create digitized historical materials from their respective collections, with emphasis on digitized books and journals. The collective project, Making of America, focused on documenting American social history from the antebellum period through Reconstruction and included approximately 5,000 books from the two collections with imprints between 1850 and 1877.

Michigan would digitize books and Cornell digitize journals related to the topic. Collectively, they expected to digitize 1.5 million page images. At both libraries, subject-specialist librarians worked closely with faculty in a variety of disciplines to identify materials that would be most useful for research and teaching needs. Not willing to risk copyright challenges, the two institutions agreed that only materials in the public domain would be included.

9. For more information, see Elsevier Science, *TULIP Final Report* (New York: Elsevier, 1996).

The University of Michigan Libraries recognized that the creation of a digital library would require intracampus collaboration, and Lougee formed alliances with the Instructional Technology division and the newly named School of Information, with engineer Daniel Atkins as its new dean. The triumvirate comprised a program committee that steered the digital library development on campus, and its success with local projects provided encouragement for taking on larger, national projects, most notably the Making of America project with Cornell and the technical framework for JSTOR, an entity created by the Mellon Foundation to digitize the scholarly journal literature, about which we write more below.

The University of Michigan was ripe for the offer that Google would make a short time later. Provost Paul Courant had decided that digitization was the answer to making collections accessible to scholars. Dean Atkins's vision for access to knowledge—and the basis of his new school—relied on digitization. Lougee had laid the groundwork and found common cause with visionaries Courant and Atkins. She realized that aligning with them was the best hope for a digital library. They had a plan; they only needed financial resources.

Libraries Shared the Dream

Other academic research libraries were not sitting by idly. Many were also experimenting with digital technology to make their collections more readily accessible. The New York Public Library launched a digitization project that made historical prints and photographs of New York widely available to the public for the first time.[10] Harvard made the decision

---

10. Deanna Marcum and Roger C. Schonfeld, interview with Paul LeClerc, August 12, 2016.

to digitize out-of-copyright monographs, but even in using student labor to digitize the books, the cost was upwards of $150 per title.[11] Michigan and Cornell secured funding from the Andrew W. Mellon Foundation to use digitization to reunite thematic collections. The University of California worked with the Internet Archive on digitization. While the goal was large-scale digitization, the approach taken had a curatorial element. It focused on public domain materials with a "subject-oriented approach focusing on popular topics." This would later evolve into a larger-scale project with funding from Microsoft.[12]

Every library, practically, recognized that the collections it held would be of interest to a far greater audience if the contents could be digitized and made available through the Internet. The topic most often discussed at professional conferences and meetings was how to secure the resources to carry out the digitization. Several research libraries used digitization as a major selling point as they recruited collections from private donors. They also asked the donors to contribute funds for digitizing the materials. The interest among libraries in digitizing their special collections prompted both the National Endowment for the Humanities and the Institute of Museum and Library Services to develop grant programs that funded their efforts. The Andrew W. Mellon Foundation started a pass-through grant program with the Council on Library and Information Resources that provided $20 million per year to be distributed to individual libraries for digitization through a competitive process.[13]

---

11. Deanna Marcum, interview with Dale Flecker, October 20, 2016.

12. Deanna Marcum and Roger C. Schonfeld, interview with Laine Farley, December 7, 2016.

13. https://www.clir.org/hiddencollections/program-history/.

Patricia Battin and the Digital Library Federation

Nearly a decade prior to the Google announcement, a group of research libraries launched a program that had the potential to develop a national digital library. To understand the relevance of this collaboration, the Digital Library Federation, it is important to review the history of the original parent organization, the Council on Library Resources.

The Council on Library Resources (CLR) was created in 1956 as a product of the Ford Foundation. Vannevar Bush, director of the Office of Scientific Research and Development, published his seminal article, "As We May Think," in the *Atlantic* in July 1945, in which he encouraged scientists to turn their attention to the "massive task of making more accessible our bewildering store of knowledge."[14] The Ford Foundation, in trying to address the problem of the proliferation of information, created CLR to "assist in attempts to discover these problems and bring the benefits of modern technology to the correction of maladjustments for which modern technology is to a large degree responsible."[15] The Ford Foundation urged the new organization it created to make grants to research libraries interested in helping solve this problem through technological means. One of the early grants CLR made was to engineering professor J.C.R. Licklider at MIT to define what the research library of 2000 would look like. In the early 1960s, long before digital technology was developed, the year 2000 seemed far away, and Licklider used the opportunity to think about "what man would like his interaction with knowledge to be."[16]

---

14. Vannevar Bush, "As We May Think," *Atlantic* 176, no. 1 (July 1945): 101–8.
15. J.C.R. Licklider, *Libraries of the Future* (Cambridge, MA: MIT Press, 1965), vi.
16. Ibid., 3.

The Council on Library Resources, from its inception, invested in preservation research and encouraged research libraries to pay special attention to its stewardship role in ensuring that scholarly resources would be available to researchers today, in ten years, and a hundred years from now. CLR was created when microfilm was a new technology, so it is not surprising that microfilming was thought to be the way to preserve scholarly content for decades to come. Vast print collections across the country, stored in libraries without any environmental controls, were becoming brittle because publishers were using acidic paper that turned to ash when exposed to changing temperatures, high humidity, and air pollution. The Council on Library Resources estimated that the task of converting acidic paper to microfilm copies would be so large that the federal government and philanthropic organizations would need to be convinced of the urgency of the problem.

CLR spun off a separate organization, the Commission on Preservation and Access, to give the initiative its undivided attention. Patricia Battin, vice president and university librarian of Columbia University, was recruited to develop a plan and to encourage collaborative action. Battin pushed for a cooperative effort, funded jointly by institutions and the National Endowment for the Humanities, that would ensure that three million of the most important scholarly monographs in the humanities would be microfilmed so that libraries everywhere could acquire copies to provide access to the materials that were too fragile to handle safely.

Digital technology was just beginning to be noticed by the library community, and a few librarians with more familiarity with technological progress scoffed at the idea that microfilming would be an appropriate preservation method in the 1980s. Why not digitize materials instead, they asked. Battin was caught between a federal agency that insisted on adhering to agreed-upon standards instead of using a new technology and the younger librarians who argued for an alternative way.

To consider the transition to the digital environment, Battin assembled a small group of some of the most forward-looking librarians to consider what would be needed for libraries to become digital libraries. The study undertaken to determine if digital preservation could become the standard was led by Donald Waters of Yale and John Garrett of CyberVillages Corporation.[17] The study they produced significantly influenced libraries across the country to begin mapping a transition to a new medium for delivering content to their readers. But perhaps the most important aspect of the study was the involvement of a new generation of librarians who would become the leaders of the digital library movement.

With funding from the Commission on Preservation and Access to start the work, several libraries banded together to form the Digital Library Federation (DLF). This new cadre of librarians developed expertise in digital technology and worked collectively to advance the state of the art. The digital leaders in the DLF-member libraries began to meet frequently to work on problems together. One of the major barriers that leaders such as John Wilkin of Michigan identified was the lack of an appropriate mechanism to coordinate a distributed effort. In particular, there was great interest in a registry that would connect digitization efforts with the print record, allowing for multiple libraries to determine their

17. Donald Waters and John Garrett, *Preserving Digital Information: Report of the Task Force on Archiving of Digital Information* (Commission on Preservation and Access, 1996), https://www.clir.org/pubs/reports/pub63/.

scanning priorities based on the work that had already taken place elsewhere.[18]

Associate librarians Donald Waters, Carol Mandel, and Wendy Lougee emerged as leaders who could easily imagine a digital future and they conducted the studies, wrote the reports, and spoke to their colleagues about how the transition could take place. Their planning for the Digital Library Federation turned into the core of digital library planning nationally. In just a short time, Waters was named the director of the DLF and later went on to assume the position of program director for scholarly communications at the Andrew W. Mellon Foundation; Mandel became Dean of Libraries at New York University; and Lougee was appointed as university librarian at the University of Minnesota. The professional bonds formed in the creation of the Digital Library Federation served them and colleague librarians well for the remainder of their careers. Their voices in their local institutions, in the Association of Research Libraries, and in the Andrew W. Mellon Foundation carried significant weight in digital developments far beyond the Digital Library Federation.

In 1997, the Council on Library Resources merged with the Commission on Preservation and Access to become the Council on Library and Information Resources (CLIR). Throughout its history, the organization focused on how technology could help men and women fundamentally rethink their relationship to and responsibility for recorded knowledge.

As an independent, nonprofit organization with no endowment, CLIR relied on sponsorship and grant funding. It had nothing more than the power of persuasion to bring to the

---

18. Deanna Marcum and Roger C. Schonfeld, interview with John Wilkin, September 27, 2016.

discussion of digital library development.[19] CLIR enjoyed the benefit of having strong support from the philanthropic community and strong board leaders from the academic community. Earlier work by the Commission on Preservation and Access had convinced the library leaders who had been working on broad preservation problems that a single focus on preservation would not be sufficient. They saw that digital technology would change virtually everything about how libraries collected, stored, and preserved research materials, and they did not believe that either the corporate or the external organizations that were working on the problem had the exclusive answer. In the earliest days of the Digital Library Federation, participating libraries believed that several of the largest and best-resourced research libraries would work cooperatively to create a distributed national digital library. They had watched as too many community-wide library collaboratives had failed to achieve their goals and so made the difficult decision that membership would be by invitation. Furthermore, they concluded that they must invest their own resources to show their level of commitment. Membership required payment of two separate fees: an annual payment of $19,000 toward the operating costs of the organization and a pledge of $25,000 to the capital fund that could be paid over five years to be used for large-scale, innovative projects. Starting with six members, DLF grew quickly to include fifteen members who signed the founding documents on May 1, 1994, at Harvard University. The governance model gave every director of participating institutions a seat on the Advisory Committee with voting privileges. Senior officers of the Research Libraries Group and OCLC

---

19. One of the authors, Deanna Marcum, served as president of CLIR from 1994 to 2002.

were invited to sit on the DLF's Advisory Committee "with voice, without vote." The Library of Congress had recently announced its intention to create a massive digital library of primary resources related to American history, and research library directors expressed concern that if the Library of Congress created a national digital library, it could undercut their own digitization efforts, or, more precisely, their efforts to raise funds for digitizing their local collections could be imperiled. The founding members invited the Library of Congress and the National Archives to join.

In an effort to bring the research library community and the Library of Congress into closer alignment, Deanna Marcum, president of the newly formed CLIR, convened a Sunday morning brunch at the Cosmos Club in June 1995 to discuss possible collaboration. Several Digital Library Federation members were joined by Librarian of Congress James Billington, who brought Jo Ann Jenkins, chief of staff, and Laura Campbell, head of the American Memory project, with him. Brian Hawkins, executive director of EDUCAUSE, also attended. The differences in perspectives were almost immediately laid bare. The Library of Congress was focused on rare and unique primary source materials. It wanted to extend its reach to make its vast collections more immediately accessible to the general population, especially to the K–12 community. Because others were digitizing books, the Library of Congress did not want to duplicate effort, the LC representatives announced. The Library of Congress had secured congressional and private funding to support its ambitious plans, and it had hired a large number of recent college graduates to process collections and digitize artifacts. EDUCAUSE had been advising the Commission on Preservation and Access on book digitization methods, and Hawkins's hope was that major libraries might be able to collaborate to achieve a massive digital library. Research librarians had come to the meeting hoping that the Library of Congress would join the efforts already under way to digitize library collections, but the research community was not the Library of Congress's focus. If the library directors had been concerned before that meeting, the discussion made clear that the Library of Congress did not consider working with the research library community a priority. The Library of Congress had its own plans and initial funding. It had made a significant political and financial investment in its American Memory digital library, and its aim was to provide historical resources for the schoolchildren of America and their teachers. Negotiating terms with the research library community would be too time-consuming and could divert scarce resources.

The major research libraries determined to work together to create a research-level digital library that served the needs of scholars and college students. Their goals and ambitions varied, however. For institutions that would later commit to Google, such as Michigan and Stanford, the focus would be on integrating Google scan files of books with internally produced scans of special collections materials. Other institutions had only begun to consider the contours of their digital libraries, and they wanted to experiment to see what worked and what did not. They were especially interested in securing grant funds that would allow them to start some kind of digital initiative.

DLF aimed to create a massive digital library to support scholarship and research. CLIR provided the organizational support for the new Digital Library Federation and hired Waters as its founding director. The decision to confine membership to those invited to join was not viewed favorably by the broader library community, and the fledgling DLF spent a great deal of time justifying its decision and fending off criticism.

Even worse, the founding members had difficulty reaching agreement on its primary purpose. Some wanted to focus on bringing their technical teams together so that the collective could make faster progress in digital library development. Some wanted to devise a distributed national digital library. Some wanted the group to be a professional development activity for the participating institutions. All of these goals could not be supported by a budget made up of contributions from fifteen members.

It is unclear whether Waters and other DLF leaders ultimately believed that a comprehensive digital library was desirable or even feasible. In 1998, Waters proposed a definition of digital libraries to which all members could subscribe, noting that a shared definition was a precursor to federating the individual libraries' holdings. The definition he created was plural: "Digital libraries are organizations that provide the resources, including the specialized staff, to select, structure, offer intellectual access to, interpret, distribute, preserve the integrity of, and ensure the persistence over time of collections of digital works so that they are readily and economically available for use by a defined community or set of communities."[20] The approach they proposed to pursue was accordingly federated.

The Digital Library Federation envisioned itself as a sunset organization; consequently, at the end of five years, a review panel was formed to evaluate the need to continue. The panel, chaired by Bernard Hurley of the University of California, Berkeley, recommended that the organization should continue through 2006, when it should undergo another evaluation. The panel considered the question of limited membership but once again concluded that the group should remain small and

20. https://old.diglib.org/about/dldefinition.htm.

suggested that the ideal size would be twenty-six to thirty-six members. The panel also called for a more structured governance and suggested that the criteria for membership should emphasize collaboration and participation.[21]

The recommendation to restrict the number of members generated further controversy in the research library community. By the time the report was published, there were thirty-seven members, leaving little room for growth. Even though collaboration was a key requirement for Digital Library Federation members, when the Google announcement broke, the five founding partners were all members of the DLF, but there had been no conversation among them to discuss terms or directions forward. The other thirty-two members of the DLF were left to wonder why they had not been included. It no longer seemed feasible, if ever it was, that the DLF would unite behind a plan for a national digital library.

William G. Bowen and JSTOR

As requests for funding came in from libraries to support all manner of digitization efforts, the Andrew W. Mellon Foundation also had digital technology in mind. It eventually settled on large-scale support for several initiatives, including Project Muse and JSTOR, among others. JSTOR is particularly instructive because it was incubated at the Mellon Foundation and championed by its president, an economist rather than a librarian.

The impetus for creating JSTOR originated at a Denison College Board of Trustees meeting in 1993. William Bowen, an

---

21. Evaluation of the Digital Library Federation, 1995–2001, Summary Report, https://old.diglib.org/about/evalrep.htm.

alumnus, and then a member of the Denison board, listened intently as President Michele Myers of the college described the overcrowded stacks of the Doane Library and asked the board to approve funding to expand the physical space. Bowen, then Mellon president, saw an opportunity to test some of the ideas he and William Baumol, a fellow economist, had offered in their definitive study of the economics of nonprofit service organizations, focusing on the arts.[22] In that study, the economists determined that these arts organizations are so labor intensive that they seem unable to take advantage of technology to do work more efficiently and thereby grow increasingly expensive to maintain over time. With that nagging finding in his bead, Bowen took special interest in the problem posed by President Myers. His coauthor, Baumol, had continued working on the economics of service organizations by taking a close look at academic libraries in 1967 and had found very similar circumstances.[23] Perhaps, Bowen thought, the overcrowded stacks of a library could be alleviated through technology rather than an expensive physical addition to the building.

With the assets of the Mellon Foundation to support his interest in using technology to advance research and scholarship, Bowen asked the foundation's secretary, Richard Ekman, and a Princeton economist who served as an advisor to the foundation, Richard E. Quandt, to run a series of experiments to determine how technology could aid in the system of scholarly communications. On December 13, 1993, Ekman and Quandt delivered their initial findings to the Mellon board.

22. William J. Baumol and William G. Bowen, *Performing Arts—the Economic Dilemma: A Study of Problems Common to Theater, Opera, Music and Dance* (New York: Twentieth Century Fund, 1966).

23. William J. Baumol and Matityahu Marcus, *Economics of Academic Libraries* (Washington, DC: American Council on Education, 1967).

Based on the paper they presented, the board approved funding for a series of "self-conscious" natural experiments to learn ways in which technology could make the system of scholarly communication more efficient and less costly. Between 1993 and 1999, the Mellon Foundation awarded grants totaling $19 million to these experimental projects.[24]

Discussions about these technology experiments led Bowen to pursue specific projects to address the library space problem. The example of Denison's Doane Library was instructive. Thousands of colleges with an emphasis on teaching undergraduates had similar collections of journals. Could computer technology be used to "miniaturize" the commonly held collections so that they could be delivered to students and faculty in digital form, alleviating the need to have the physical copy on the shelves? A study by the Denison University Library staff found that the journals occupied 23 percent of space, and government documents occupied another 13 percent.[25] At the national level, President Clinton had addressed the government documents problem by signing a law that ordered the distribution of government-produced information in digital form. The scholarly journals presented the best opportunity for further experimentation with digital technology for colleges and universities.

Journals posed a significant challenge in that they were copyright protected, but unlike books that have complicated copyright arrangements that involve authors, publishers, and literary estates, journals' copyrights are typically held by the

---

24. Roger C. Schonfeld, *JSTOR: A History* (Princeton: Princeton University Press, 2003), 8.
25. Ibid., 9.

publisher alone. Bowen was willing to make the necessary arrangements with journal publishers to allow the new entity he created, JSTOR, to digitize the content and make it available in digital form. Libraries had already adopted the idea that miniaturization could help them manage space by buying microfilmed copies of journals for their collections. Libraries had experience with vendors (mostly University Microfilms, Inc.) that made arrangements with large research libraries to film their collections that would subsequently be sold as microfilm versions to other libraries. As much as librarians appreciated the virtues of microfilm editions of journals, students hated to use them and, consequently, did so only under duress. The possibility of digital technology opened up many new and creative ways of making the content easily and readily accessible to students.

The Mellon Foundation's business was to make grants to academic institutions, so Bowen needed to find a college or university that would be interested enough in the possibility of digitized journals to apply for a grant. Bowen engaged Ira Fuchs, Princeton University's vice president for Computing and Information Technology, in the project and urged him to develop the best technical plan for proceeding. Bowen had assumed that CD-ROMs, then the prevailing digital technology, would be the distribution medium for digitized journals, but Fuchs promoted thinking about a networked approach. Eventually, they established a partnership with the University of Michigan, where technology developed as part of the TULIP partnership would be adapted for use by JSTOR. They found a willing partner in Richard DeGennaro, then the Roy Larsen Librarian of Harvard College. Harvard had already embarked on a plan for digitizing thirty titles by creating a database of page images that could be searched by Harvard faculty and students. Because the materials would not be available beyond Harvard's walls, the library expected to rely on fair use exemptions of the copyright law for making digitized content available on the campus.

Bowen, an economist who always reminded colleagues that nothing is free, took the position that by seeking permission from publishers to digitize and distribute content, there were good prospects for developing a self-sustaining business model. The Mellon Foundation provided early funding for the development of JSTOR, always with the idea that it would become an economically viable organization. Although JSTOR did not ever purport to be a freely accessible, open library of journal content, its great contribution was demonstrating that mass digitization was possible. As libraries began to offer JSTOR to their faculty and students, and seeing their users' enthusiasm for digital resources, all libraries began thinking about other parts of the library that could be made digital.

The most interesting aspect of JSTOR's creation is that it applied digitization to an important library problem: overcrowded shelves of print journals, which led to an outcome that was both better and less expensive. The process of identifying a collection of journals to be digitized, securing agreements from publishers to carry out the digitization, and making those available to libraries in a format that made research much easier for scholars and students proved to be an enormously valuable proof of concept. At the same time, it freed up space in libraries that could be used for other purposes, saving capital and operating costs. JSTOR was evidence that libraries could use technology to deliver new and valuable services. It was also clear that much more work needed to be done. As valuable as JSTOR was for making journal content more readily available, it was not a comprehensive effort to build a digital library.

For Mellon, the JSTOR investment was transformative. It illustrated the potential of digital investments in the library sector, and it led Bowen to establish a new program area focused on libraries and scholarly communication. In 1999, Mellon recruited Waters to develop this new program. For more than twenty years, Waters's leadership would shape not only Mellon's substantial grant making but also many elements of academia's strategy for digitization and library investments broadly.

Commercializing Special Collections

The American Antiquarian Society is the foremost collection of early Americana, sponsoring an array of research and educational programs on the field. Its collections would be widely valued if digitized and made more widely available. But like many other special collections, it lacked the expertise and resources to consider its own digitization and digital delivery infrastructure. Such organizations in many cases partnered with a third party, such as Readex, ProQuest, or Gale.

These partnerships varied to some degree but they often had a series of common elements. The third party (often a commercial organization) would cover the upfront costs of digitization and then have an exclusive period during which it alone could include the digitized materials in e-resources that would be licensed to libraries across the country and around the world. The originating special collection would receive a fee, often during the extent of the exclusive period, as well as the digitized outputs (such as page images from scanned books), which after the period of exclusivity could be repurposed.

These arrangements addressed a variety of interests. They vastly increased access to the underlying special collections materials. They provided a revenue stream to the special collection that had taken responsibility for acquiring and preserving the materials. And they provided a return on invested capital to the third party, without which neither of these benefits might have been possible. At the same time, because of the nature of the commercial partnership, they did not provide broad open access to materials, most of which were out of copyright.

A Widely Shared Dream

Digitization and network technology allowed a variety of different dreamers to see real possibilities of being able to make library collections easily and freely accessible. Previously, librarians had focused on making discovery information available—abstracts, indexes, cataloging records, and collection guides. This was an enormous contribution to discovery and access, but library processes and procedures still stood between the knowledge sources and their users. With the advent of digitization and the Internet, dreamers could realistically imagine a comprehensive digital library that all scholars and students could use at anytime from anywhere. They simply needed infusions of cash, technology, and partnerships to allow them to move ahead.

Librarians dreamed of a library-centered transformation, one that would elevate their expertise and bring their curatorial approach to millions of new users. By contrast, business leaders and computer scientists did not necessarily envision that an information-rich future would depend upon the traditional libraries at all. The computer and its access to the Internet would be the new library for all.

The two groups tried to work together in many instances; in others, they proceeded more separately. The need to bring together contributions from both parties may be clear in retrospect. But at the time, each of these grand experiments faced organizational limitations of one type or another. The dream was compelling; the way to achieve it remained elusive.

3

A Stunning Announcement

LIBRARIES JUMP ON BOARD

In the 1990s, librarians and technologists pursued a number of important efforts to digitize content on a large enough scale to create digital libraries. Some of these resulted in viable products or businesses, while others can best be characterized as demonstration projects, but none created a universal library or transformed the nature of the research library. Then, in October 2004, a commercial start-up company made an announcement that changed the course of digitization and digital library development. Google focused its attention on digitizing collections of knowledge at an unprecedented scale and with unprecedented speed, bringing the technology, organizational skills, talent, and money to do the job. Even though Google was a relatively new company, it had gained recognition as an effective search engine, and its ambitious founders, Sergey Brin and Larry Page, were already receiving intense media attention and always looking for the next big thing.

From its creation, Google portrayed itself as an organization concerned about doing good. At the time, the user community was generally negative about Microsoft, and many complained about the company's monopolistic approach to product bundling. Google's slogan "don't be evil" responded to that criticism of Microsoft, but it also signaled the optimistic attitude of the young founders, who seemed determined to make the world better. Google's vision was "to organize the world's information and make it universally accessible," which conveniently enough also served the interests of the advertising-driven business model that would propel the company and its founders to unimaginable riches. Having organized all the world's websites and made them discoverable through its basic search product, Google imagined the benefits to society of having the world's knowledge that is contained in books as part of the discovery process. Brin and Page were also dreamers who wanted to make the world's information universally accessible. In 2004–5, they launched several major programs that would significantly change the nature of book discovery and usage and, in the process, changed the nature of research libraries.

Google Print

Google first announced an initiative to work with publishers, indexing the content of recently published books while offering a new, free service that would digitize frontlist books and make them discoverable and purchasable. It would allow simultaneous searches of "billions of web pages and texts of hundreds of thousands of books" to find information about all manner of subjects and enable the book-buying public to easily make purchases. This service would also enhance the already robust

Google index of websites by adding digitized books that had been made available to Google by the publisher. What better place to make their historic announcement than at the Frankfurt Book Fair, the largest annual international gathering of publishers that traces its history to the Gutenberg era? At the point of the public announcement, a number of major publishers, including Houghton Mifflin, Scholastic, and Penguin, had signed on to participate. Google cofounders Brin and Page made a personal appearance at the October 2004 book fair, reminding participants that Google's mission was to "organize the world's information and make it accessible," with books a natural next step to complement web search.[1]

Dubbed Google Print, the service would allow a user to search across the catalogs of all participating publishers, including the full text of the books in those catalogs. When searchers found topics of interest referenced in a book, they could view a relevant but limited number of pages. Google Print would include links to online retailers from which the book could be purchased, perhaps eventually allowing them to take out retailers as the middlemen. Publishers did not pay to participate. Indeed, Google promised to share the revenue it earned from selling advertising with the publishers.

This idea was not entirely new; it had certain similarities to Amazon's Look Inside the Book, which eventually became Search Inside the Book, features that allowed potential customers

---

1. Edward Wyatt, "New Google Service May Strain Old Ties in Bookselling," *New York Times*, October 8, 2004, C3, http://www.nytimes.com/2004/10/08/technology /new-google-service-may-strain-old-ties-in-bookselling.html. The mission statement of Google, interestingly enough, was similar to the mission the Library of Congress used in 2004: sustaining, preserving, and making accessible its universal collections: http://lcweb2.loc.gov/master/libn/about/reports-and-budgets/documents/annual -reports/fy2004.pdf.

to read a few pages of a book before purchasing. Amazon had already established a foothold as a bookseller, even though its online sales had deleterious effects on brick-and-mortar bookstores and a growing market concentration that was frightening to publishers. Publishers expressed concern about the possibility of a single book distributor, and even though the Amazon Kindle and the e-book era it launched were still in the future, publishers seized on the opportunity to foster competition among the Internet giants to lessen the likelihood of a future with only a single distributor. Dan Clancy, Google's lead on the Google project, credited publishers' willingness to participate in Google Print because they "were always concerned about the central power of Amazon."[2] The *New York Times* reported that "Google Print, the new search engine that allows consumers to search the content of books online, could help touch off an important shift in the balance of power between companies that produce books and those that sell them."[3] Although publishers expressed some tentative concerns that this new service had to protect copyright, they were vocal in their support for Google Print, at least as they understood it at the time. Clancy recalled that "publishers liked this because it would help them sell more books. It was a complement to what Amazon was already doing."[4] But, as we will explain later, for publishers, there were concerns beyond simply wanting to sell more books.

Google's early plans for the project differed somewhat from what eventually emerged. Google thought the first logical step would be to secure collaborative agreements with publishers.

---

2. Deanna Marcum, interview with Dan Clancy, April 13, 2016.
3. Wyatt, "New Google Service May Strain Old Ties in Bookselling."
4. Clancy, interview.

As Dan Clancy explained: "If we wanted to make [scanned books] accessible for people to look at content, we would need to get agreements from copyright holders. The idea was to go to publishers and get permission to show part of the book. Early on, there were two parts to our project: the library project, where we scan public domain material, and the publisher project, where we got copyright holder permission and put the book through a sheet scanner—higher quality and cheaper."[5] But the library project was unknown at the time and would eventually become more ambitious than simply referencing public domain material.

Indeed, when Google Print and its publisher partnerships were announced at Frankfurt, the publishers did not know that Google was also making quiet forays into major research libraries to convince them to allow Google to digitize their collections—the retrospective record of knowledge contained in books. Publishers were generally supportive when they thought they were Google's sole partners. When they learned that libraries would be the source of not only public domain books but also in some cases in-copyright materials, they were surprised and had serious concerns.

Google seems to have imagined that the lines between in-copyright and public domain were more simply and clearly drawn. Google assumed that it could make agreements with publishers for materials under copyright and simply digitize out-of-print materials through library partnerships, as if there was a bright line between the two.[6] Librarians and publishers

5. Ibid.
6. Barbara Quint, "Google and Research Libraries Launch Massive Digitization Project," *Information Today*, December 20, 2004, http://newsbreaks.infotoday.com /NewsBreaks/Google-and-Research-Libraries-Launch-Massive-Digitization-Project -16307.asp.

saw far greater complexity about what was in or out of print and about orphan works, and therefore were far less confident that Google's publisher agreements alone could actually cover all the in-copyright materials, even for those publishers' books. These complexities—and Google's naivete about or indifference to them—in trying to build toward comprehensiveness drew Google into enormous tension with the publisher and author communities and ultimately would prevent this ambitious project from achieving its goals.

A Healthy Disregard for the Impossible

Google's ambitions were great: it aspired to organize all the world's information. But achieving such a brash goal was more than a little complicated: at the time much of that information was not available online. It would be difficult to characterize Google as the source of the world's knowledge if it contained only the websites that existed in 2004–5. Dan Clancy recalled Google's interest quickly turned to "offline information," which its leaders "needed to digitize so they could index it."[7] To serve the needs of Google's users, looking for massive amounts of content, offline information, including library books, would need to be digitized and made discoverable.

But Google's interests were also more abstract. Larry Page was a driving force behind the library digitization project at Google. His organization was in its infancy, but he talked passionately about distinguishing this new Silicon Valley start-up by moving from a more purely technology focus to an expanding interest in information and knowledge that could have a significant impact on the world.

7. Clancy, interview.

At the highest levels, the mind-set was profoundly utopian. Michael Keller remembers participating in a gathering that Paul Allen hosted at his estate in the San Juan Islands to address the question of "the final encyclopedia," which would be developed by a new-age "monastic order" that could be trusted to gather "all of the information that ever was or would be" on some kind of "large satellite" from which it could be shared widely to "make it possible for all citizens in the cosmos to make good decisions." Larry Page was among the participants. The messianic optimism that must have undergirded the discussion at Allen's salon introduces into our narrative a different element than the traditional discussions about revenue, market share, and profitability that might inform more quotidian corporate decision making.[8]

If Google were to advance this dream, Google founders Brin and Page needed books to digitize, and not just the books that publishers were currently selling but all those that had been published in history. Perhaps librarians could be persuaded to partner with Google to accomplish the task. The Google entrepreneurs were relatively recent graduates of the University of Michigan and Stanford University. Fortunately, the directors of those libraries also happened to be entrepreneurial risk-takers. They had tried—individually and in partnership with others— to initiate mass digitization programs in their own institutions, but limited resources had constrained the efforts. An approach from Google came at an opportune time in each of the institutions, especially in light of the plans of the libraries. From the broader institutional perspective, there was strong interest in developing relationships with these two stars of Silicon Valley whose creativity promised to yield strong financial results.

8. Deanna Marcum, interview with Michael Keller, March 15, 2017.

Page spoke directly, and separately, with Michigan and Stanford. As a Michigan alumnus, and as one of the wealthiest individuals in the world, Page had a complex relationship with his alma mater. He served as a member of the external advisory committee of the Engineering School. Later, he would receive an honorary doctorate from the university, recalling in his speech to graduates that he learned at Michigan to have a "healthy disregard for the impossible."[9] It clearly served him well in advancing the Google book digitization program.

The Michigan Partnership

The Michigan partnership was unique because it involved digitizing essentially the university's entire general collection. When Page "offered to digitize our entire collection,"[10] according to Provost Paul Courant, the university responded with gusto. Courant recognized that if they were left to their own resources, Michigan librarians would take more than a thousand years to digitize the library's seven million volumes using existing approaches and their internal budgets. Google aimed to complete the project in six years.[11] Courant reacted unambiguously when he first learned about the proposal: "I thought that was a good idea."[12]

Courant had been following the digital developments at the library quite closely, as he believed that digital technology

9. A video and transcript of his speech at that event are available at http://googlepress.blogspot.com/2009/05/larry-pages-university-of-michigan.html.

10. Courant, interview.

11. Katie Hafner, "At Harvard, a Man, a Plan and a Scanner," *New York Times*, November 21, 2015, http://www.nytimes.com/2005/11/21/business/at-harvard-a-man-a-plan-and-a-scanner.html.

12. Courant, interview.

would solve many of the economic and space problems that plagued the library. From his perspective, he would later recall, it seemed that the library's project, while promising, would be a long, slow process. He was encouraged when he learned that Google might have an interest in helping. Courant recalled his first encounter with Google this way:

> The College of Engineering had invited alumnus Larry Page to visit the campus. This was somewhere in the 2002–4 period. It is important to remember that at this stage, Google wasn't big. It had not gone public. It was not a great force of the modern economy. This was an amiable $2 million a year enterprise run by two Silicon Valley guys. The company was a very sharp, hip "comer"—no one thought of it as we know it today. Larry Page, while on campus, approached the dean of the Engineering College and asked if he could talk with the university librarian. The dean invited then librarian Bill Gosling to come to the Engineering College to talk with Page. Within a day of that meeting, Larry Page, Bill Gosling, and John Wilkin [associate librarian for technology] showed up in my office and told me that Larry Page had offered to digitize our entire collection. I thought that was a good idea. I asked if it would cost us anything. What requirements would Google impose on us? My interest was in the quality of the scans that Google would produce. From the beginning, we had preservation in mind. Having a digital backup in the library would help us with the enormous problem of paper deterioration.[13]

The University of Michigan and Google needed each other. The provost saw great benefit to moving ahead more expeditiously with digitization; Google needed a willing partner.

13. Ibid.

Michigan brought together a library with existing experience and expertise in digitization, technology, and preservation, at a university already thinking in ambitious terms about the transformative power of digital initiatives, with strong leaders willing to take some measured risks in partnership with a wealthy alumnus.

Even so, it is difficult to imagine the Google book digitization project taking hold as successfully as it did at the University of Michigan if Paul Courant had not been there. Courant was one of those rare university leaders who had served in several capacities: professor, budget officer, acting librarian, and provost, even repeating some of them. He had deep knowledge of the University of Michigan and its culture and practices, and he understood the need for libraries to address their digital future.

Certain key aspects of the relationship between the libraries and Google were established in discussions between Michigan and Google. For Courant, having the university receive a digital file of all the materials that Google proposed to digitize was a critical factor, not least to ensure that it would be able to provide digital access to its own campus and community. "My immediate question was how would we use a digital copy," recalled Courant. "We very quickly told Page that we wanted our own digital copy. He asked why, but we insisted on our own copy."[14] While the contract was being negotiated, Michigan added a provision that would allow it to use its digital copy not only for local purposes but also "as part of services offered in

---

14. Ibid. This decision would later become an area of contention for publishers, who understood clearly that this was a key part of the quid pro quo for the libraries. "Why did Google want to give the files to the libraries? Libraries would not have participated. One hundred percent. Libraries wanted archival copies at least of everything in their collection. Many aspired to something more than that." Deanna Marcum and Roger C. Schonfeld, interview with Richard Sarnoff, August 30, 2016.

cooperation with partner research libraries such as the institutions of the Digital Library Federation."[15]

While digitization efforts had advanced tremendously in recent years and the utopian ideals of making all information digitally available were widely discussed, digitizing an entire research library collection had never before been seriously proposed. This was something new: a strong technology partner with the deep pockets and audacious mind-set to try to make something tangible happen and two library leaders willing to take big risks in order to achieve their goals.

Perhaps because they were more accustomed to working transparently because of their public institution status, or because the institution had already developed a plan for a digital library, Paul Courant and his Michigan colleagues thought more creatively and expansively than other institutions in their negotiations with Google. Book digitization for them was a means to building a digital library that could be preserved. They could use Google's investment to catapult the library into the digital era.

At the same time, the actual decision-making process at Michigan was steeped in secrecy rather than following normal processes. Courant believed that a decision of this magnitude should go to the university's regents, but to keep the conversation bounded, the issue was not discussed by the faculty library committee. He knew that faculty would object to being excluded, but Courant understood that certain legal and other issues had to be approved at the highest levels before the University of Michigan could proceed with Google. Wilkin remembers some agonizing about whether Michigan should

---

15. The cooperative agreement is available online at http://www.lib.umich.edu /sites/default/files/services/mdp/um-google-cooperative-agreement.pdf.

participate, with a decision coming down to "if we don't do this, somebody else will, and if we don't have some say and control I think we are going to regret it."[16]

The dynamics of how the first wave of participants was developed and announced is interesting, not least because the very fact that Google was discussing digitization with these libraries was kept under wraps prior to the public announcement. There were multiple reasons Google wanted to keep the negotiations secret. Perhaps most important among them was to avoid news of the library digitization deal leaking out to publishers. Presumably, were this to happen, it could have negatively affected its negotiations with publishers for the October 2004 Google Print announcement.[17]

As a result of the secrecy in the project, Michigan was for some time not aware that other libraries were involved. Courant recalled, "We had no idea they were talking to others."[18] Over time, they began to learn that others were involved and made contact, but they could not negotiate as a group. They learned that Google "would have phone calls with the other [potential] partners saying, if you don't sign we'll go along with just Michigan. . . . Google wanted not to be locked in with a single institution—things weren't always easy with us" as Michigan worked to hold Google to the scanning standards it

16. Wilkin, interview.

17. Michigan was certainly clear about this: "Our partner (Google) does not want information about the [library digitization] project shared beyond key individuals for several months. They have a variety of reasons for this; a central one is that they are in negotiation with several publishers and do not want early information to damage their negotiations." John Wilkin, memorandum to Don Waters and Kevin Guthrie, "Overview of cooperative repository concept," May 20, 2004, offices of ITHAKA Harbors, New York.

18. Courant, interview.

sought to establish.[19] None of this is especially unusual in a multiparty negotiation. But it may raise questions about whether the libraries involved were adequately positioned to negotiate with a strategically sophisticated counterparty like Google.

Libraries have a long tradition of collaborating to make collections widely available to the scholarly community. They customarily informed their collaborating colleagues about decisions they were contemplating. The nondisclosure agreements reached with a large and highly visible corporate partner marked a new chapter in librarianship history, and the benefits as well as the challenges of such partnerships would be the subject of conference papers, articles, and hallway conversation for years to come.

Scanning and Standards

A partnership with libraries introduced new issues to the project. Over the course of 2003, Google and Michigan discussed issues related to technical standards and scanning practices extensively. Two key related considerations presented themselves. First, Michigan, from the outset, saw digitization as a preservation strategy. To ensure that scans were of high enough quality to meet preservation standards, the university expected to review the fidelity, resolution, and other aspects of the scanning outputs and have final approval authority. Michigan's standards focused on "human readability" and discoverability of content. Second was the nature of the scanning process itself.[20] As Courant emphasized in his interview, he was obsessed with

---

19. Wilkin, interview.
20. This issue was explored at some length and explained in an e-mail from John Wilkin to the library's executive leadership group on March 11, 2003.

good-quality scans, as he knew the University of Michigan faculty would revolt if they were presented poor-quality library resources with which they were to carry out their research.[21] Previous to the Google initiative, there were two principal ways to scan a book. In the first the volume would be guillotined and pages fed through a high-speed scanner, with the non-trivial disadvantage that the book would be damaged and require rebinding if it were not destroyed and deaccessioned altogether. In the second, a book would be placed in a cradle that allowed it to be held open while an operator manually photographed the volume on a page-by-page basis, with the disadvantages of a slower process that brought the curvature of the pages into the scan. Google developed and eventually patented an approach that realized the speed of the first approach with the non-destructiveness of the second approach.

Along the way, Google also explored the possibility of a partnership with the not-for-profit Internet Archive, also interested in scanning books and increasing their discoverability and availability. But ultimately, Google concluded that it could drive the cost down farther on its own. Dan Clancy recalls that the Internet Archive and its leader, Brewster Kahle, would have offered a solution that "was three times more expensive than us. His method would have cost a billion dollars."[22] The failure to reach agreement on a partnership arrangement led Kahle to develop a competing system, leaving Google to perfect its scanning technology to keep costs low. Google's actual costs for scanning have not been shared, but even if Google reduced Internet Archive's costs by two-thirds, as Clancy believes, its investment was considerable.

21. Courant, interview.
22. Clancy, interview.

Google engineers began working with Michigan to develop and implement the specific plans for the scanning operations. A bit of library trivia explains one of the reasons why Michigan was especially well suited to participate as a partner: the design of its off-site storage facility. At the time, many such off-site facilities had been designed to assign books into boxes to fit the most into a given box, and these boxes were in turn stored in a warehouse-style facility, using a unique barcode on the box to identify its location in the warehouse at any given time. The books were not in any fixed location and following a circulation could be reshelved where it was most convenient. The books were organized via an inventory management system. But Michigan's facility stored books by size, which made it possible to set up a scanning workflow by size. In addition, Michigan librarians convinced Google to extract the cataloging data associated with each item's barcode, rather than trying to extract all metadata from the book scans themselves.[23]

Google quickly discovered that meeting library standards required more effort than it first thought, and the company had to make a number of improvements to both the scanning setup and process. On metadata and markup, Google chose to dramatically reduce the amount of processing for library digitization initiatives. From a process perspective, Google's initial innovations included attaching each of two cameras (one for the verso and one for the recto pages) to separate computers, significantly improving speed. There was also no processing during the scanning procedure itself. Processing would take place later in Google's data centers, and materials could be reprocessed over time as OCR and other algorithms improved.[24]

23. Wilkin, interview.
24. Ibid.

Wilkin recalls that "there was a time where only 50 percent of the files were meeting our specifications." Google wanted to ensure an adequate level of quality to enable searching. Michigan recognized that "this is so different from a collection/format migration/preservation perspective," and it was aggressive in enforcing this aspect of its agreement. "The fidelity issue was probably the point of greatest tension. They wanted to back away from that—it was hard for them—and we pushed back. When things broke down on the image quality issue it took a phone call including Larry Page among others to resolve."[25]

In an earlier experiment launched at the Library of Congress, the staff concluded that the quality of scans was not high enough for it to accept. The University of Michigan was more accepting of Google's end product. The university was concerned about the guillotining of books, and although the scanning methodology in the end was non-destructive, Michigan librarians would have gone ahead with the project regardless. There was a willingness in the library to allow at least some amount of disbinding, on a case-by-case basis. In explaining this thinking, Wilkin was careful to remind his colleagues that "Michigan will be using these images not only for access purposes but also for preservation purposes," as was the case with previous, more bespoke projects.[26]

On April 19, 2004, well before the publisher partnership was even announced, Michigan and Google signed the first collaboration agreement, a six-month pilot (subsequently extended) to allow them to move forward together. The scanning technology and the outputs produced were tested beginning in June.

25. Ibid.

26. This issue was explored at some length and explained in an e-mail from John Wilkin to the library's executive leadership group on March 11, 2003.

Production initially began in October 2004. Because Michigan had preservation as a goal, library standards and processes became the norm for the Google book digitization project.

Even while efforts developed on the scanning front, there were open questions on how the ultimate "product" would be structured, that is, how Google would provide access to the digitized files for users. One model was for the libraries themselves to provide access through a multi-institution digital repository that Wilkin was already discussing with colleagues in the Committee on Institutional Cooperation (a consortium that mainly consisted of Big Ten institutions). The model of providing access through a library repository would have the advantage of enabling the libraries to control the "canonical" digital delivery copy and provide a mechanism for non-Google-digitized library holdings to be crawled by Google's search engine. Although Google might have been willing to pay some of the cost of such a library repository, it would have wanted it to hold color image files, which from Wilkin's perspective would have raised the cost to a prohibitive level.[27] This option was abandoned and Google itself would ultimately provide access to the digital files.

Announcing the Library Partnership

Google's announcement of the partnership with libraries was released in December 2004, just a few months after its publisher partnership announcement. At the time, Google took the approach of setting a date for a product announcement, working backward from there to build it, and then announcing the project at whatever state of development it had achieved. Five

---

27. Wilkin, memorandum.

libraries—Michigan, Stanford, Harvard, the New York Public Library, and Oxford University—were on board. And, although other options may have been considered, the service that was announced involved Google hosting the content and providing access to snippets for in-copyright material and complete works for public domain items.[28]

The announcement of the library project was quickly termed "mass digitization." While libraries had thus far taken a curated approach to digitization and had scanned based on a bibliography or a particular topic, Google proposed to scan everything. The specifics of what was to be scanned varied among the partner institutions. Michigan was unique in its focus on having digitized files returned for its local use. A full cooperative agreement was finally signed on June 15, 2005.[29] Michigan was unique in another way: it was the only public university in the initial announcement, and therefore the only institution that would need to make the contract with Google available for public inspection.[30]

Google made another contribution: it took an engineering approach to library processing. In its purest form, Google would have systematically worked its way through the stacks of a library, scanning every item on the shelves. Its project leaders had calculated its costs to be lower in digitizing a given work twice than to identify potential duplication in advance and avoid it. The project's appetite was thus not only voracious

---

28. This distinction between public domain and in-copyright materials does not appear in the initial news coverage of, for example, the *New York Times* and *San Francisco Chronicle* but can be found within a week: Quint, "Google and Research Libraries Launch Massive Digitization Project."

29. Wilkin, interview.

30. Courant, interview.

but seemingly even unlimited, entirely as a result of the economics at a technical level.

At first glance, Google's plan had something for everyone. The company expected to scan every book in five large, comprehensive libraries, yielding ten million scanned books. The scanned books would be indexed, but the search results would be rendered in different ways. Public domain works would be available in their entirety, rendered page by page. For those books that were still in print, Google promised to work with publishers to determine what parts of their books would be accessible and under what conditions, presumably following the principles of the publisher partnership.

The coverage of the announcement was positive. There was little critical examination of why Google would pursue such an initiative. One Google executive explained neutrally that the ability to search books would draw more users to its services: "We know adding a lot more information to our search index will make the search experience more useful, leading to more searches. Having more searches will lead to more revenue."[31]

The *New York Times* noticed that there could be competition in the book digitization arena. Its coverage speculated that "because the Google agreements are not exclusive, the pacts are almost certain to touch off a race with other major Internet search providers like Amazon, Microsoft and Yahoo."[32] Indeed, Keller recalls that at Stanford, "We approached Amazon and

---

31. Carolyn Said, "Revolutionary Chapter/Google's Ambitious Book-Scanning Plan Seen as Key Shift in Paper-Based Culture," *San Francisco Chronicle*, December 20, 2004, http://www.sfgate.com/business/article/Revolutionary-chapter-Google-s -ambitious-2662491.php.

32. See, for example, John Markoff and Edward Wyatt, "Google Is Adding Major Libraries to Its Database," *New York Times*, December 14, 2004, http://www.nytimes .com/2004/12/14/technology/google-is-adding-major-libraries-to-its-database.html.

Yahoo and Microsoft and we would make deals with them, too. We had good conversations with Amazon, but in the end, they decided that they were not going to get into that business."[33] Publishers expressed tentative support for the library digitization initiative, seeing it as an extension of the existing publisher partnership.[34] This would shift dramatically in a relatively short period of time, as we explore at length in chapter 5.

The Initial Partners

Months before the Google announcement was made, the company first approached the Library of Congress about the possibility of digitizing its collections. After an initial experiment with Google to digitize law books, the library concluded that the quality of the scans was not acceptable. More importantly, the leadership worried that Google's stance on copyright contradicted the policies of the U.S. Copyright Office (an official part of the Library of Congress) and it would not be wise for the national library to enter into a relationship with a commercial company. Google then looked to major research libraries as potential partners. In terms of scale, the original announcement of the Google Print for Libraries program was remarkable, stunning even. The five initial libraries held approximately one-third of all the book titles known to be held by all libraries, as recorded in OCLC's WorldCat database.[35] Although plans for digitization in several of the libraries were selective rather than comprehensive, over time other library partners would be

33. Keller, interview.

34. Quint, "Google and Research Libraries Launch Massive Digitization Project."

35. Brian Lavoie, Lynn Silipigni Connaway, and Lorcan Dempsey, "Anatomy of Aggregate Collections: The Example of Google Print for Libraries," *D-Lib Magazine*, September 2005, available at https://www.dllib.org/dlib/september05/lavoie/09lavoie.html.

added and a substantial share of the published record would be digitized through this program.

At the time of the public announcement, the libraries were participating on a very different basis from one another. The University of Michigan—the only organization among the original five that was an organ of a state government—was the only one that would commit from the beginning to digitize its entire collection ("excluding its rare books and other fragile material") of seven million books.[36] Michigan was perhaps most focused on the public purpose, based on internal documents we have been able to review.

The Stanford track proceeded more or less in parallel with that of Michigan. Page invited Stanford's university librarian, Michael Keller, whom he and Brin had known since graduate school, to a meeting at their offices, the "Googleplex," in 2003, with Stanford professor Terry Winograd. As Keller recalls, "Larry said he wanted to digitize all books in the world. He asked if Stanford would like to do that. I said yes."[37] Stanford and Harvard both held out hope that they might digitize on a similar, or greater, scale, to that of Michigan. Stanford, the other participating university with a direct connection to Google and its founders, would begin by making a substantial two-million-book commitment but eventually expected to digitize its eight-million-book general collection. By 2019, approximately 3.5 million volumes had been digitized. Stanford's Keller reflects that "we did the Google project to increase the ROI on printed works at Stanford. . . . All along, my intention was to have a massive text base here for research for the Stanford faculty."[38]

36. Quint, "Google and Research Libraries Launch Massive Digitization Project."
37. Keller, interview.
38. Ibid.

Harvard's pilot was smaller yet, a commitment of 40,000 books but holding out the prospect that its entire 15-million-volume collection would be digitized via this project.[39] Harvard antici-pated that by the time public domain items had been scanned Google would have reached an agreement with publishers to continue into in-copyright materials.[40]

The final two announced from the beginning that they would only be permitting the digitization of public domain materi-als. Oxford's contributions would be restricted to nineteenth-century materials, old enough to be out of copyright, fragile enough to merit digitization and greater care of the original artifacts, and yet not housed in environmentally controlled conditions.[41]

The New York Public Library restricted its participation to out-of-copyright but non-fragile materials. Then-president Paul LeClerc recalls that "the internal decision making didn't really have much lack of clarity about whether NYPL wanted to participate. . . . The reason it was important to work with Google was that we couldn't raise the money to digitize that many books."[42]

Later in the project, dozens more libraries would join Google's digitization initiative. Over time, libraries would not choose which collections to digitize, nor would Google take a shelf-clearing approach. Mike Furlough, then at Penn State, recalls that "by the time Google got to Penn State, there was not a lot of strategy involved. They were working from a pick list."[43] They were filling in the missing pieces of an increasingly

39. Quint, "Google and Research Libraries Launch Massive Digitization Project."
40. Flecker, interview.
41. Quint, "Google and Research Libraries Launch Massive Digitization Project."
42. LeClerc, interview.
43. Deanna Marcum, interview with Mike Furlough, May 25, 2016.

comprehensive digital collection. During the early years of the Google book digitization project, the corporation grew quickly. No longer a small start-up, Google had become synonymous with easy searching for information. Some libraries worried that they had ceded control to a corporation. Others celebrated the investment that Google was making in their big goal: to build a digital library.

Google Strategy

The influences that drew Google into books were wide-ranging. For one, there were the utopian dreams shared by some technology visionaries that translated into Google's business goal of indexing all the world's information, regardless of format. There is reason to believe that Google used the digitized books in developing and training various artificial intelligence algorithms. And there were also clear competitive and product goals worth considering.

First, Google already saw Amazon as a competitor, increasingly so as the two companies' strategies would continue to develop. Allying with publishers and libraries to develop alternatives to Amazon's growing dominance of the book business was a savvy move.

Second, it is perhaps more than a coincidence that Google Scholar, the free service that would take a dominant position in discovery of scientific journal articles, was announced at almost the same time as Google's book initiatives. Did Google intend to build up its presence, perhaps envisioning creating an academic information service over time?

While Google's strategic motivations remain only partially understandable, it is clear that the company would have found its goals far harder to achieve at scale without the strong partnership with the University of Michigan. In the end, Michigan provided the plurality of the books that Google would digitize and was the only library whose general collection was digitized completely. This provided an enormous boost to the project, and it positioned Michigan as the most digital research library in the world.

4

Unlocking Access

The announcement of the Google book digitization project was striking. While many had long seen the benefits of digitizing the intellectual and cultural heritage contained in the millions of books held by major research libraries, the number of digitized books that were accessible to the public remained pitifully small. Google and its partners expressed their intention to make books widely available, and in relatively short order. The biggest beneficiaries of the Google book digitization project stood to be those outside academia—individuals who previously had at best limited access to the long tail of society's cultural and intellectual heritage. Mass digitization stood to make a meaningful, if incomplete, improvement in this access. Many were enthusiastic about the possibility.

Existing Conditions

The Google book digitization project announcement, like the work of the dreamers profiled in chapter 2, sought to address inequities in access to cultural and intellectual heritage. These inequities were unintended. They were the product of the substantial investment that the academic sector in the United States—led by its research universities—had made in acquiring a vast wealth of materials not only domestically but worldwide in support of local priorities for research and scholarship.[1]

Over time, universities would compete with one another, not only abstractly for prestige but directly for students and faculty members, based in part on the collections that their libraries had assembled. But they also shared them robustly with one another, and to some extent with public libraries, using the interlibrary lending networks discussed in chapter 1. Discovery tools and reference services were also far more well developed at the major research libraries. For these reasons, inequities in using this long tail of collections—at both the discovery and access levels—had developed.

The inequities in access to materials widely accessible within academia did not cover only printed books. For example, scientific journals containing the latest research were readily available at major scientific institutions, such as research universities, but were more selectively available at smaller colleges and hardly at all at public libraries, primarily for reasons of cost. Discovery systems for these journals were also more readily available at the institutions that conducted the largest volume of scientific research. Vast amounts of scientific and medical research, even that which was government

---

1. See the history of collecting and preservation presented here: Stephen G. Nichols and Abby Smith, *The Evidence in Hand: Report of the Task Force on the Artifact in Library Collections* (Washington, DC: Council on Library and Information Resources, 2001), http://www.clir.org/pubs/reports/pub103/pub103.pdf, 53, 70. See also Roger C. Schonfeld, "Taking Stock: Sharing Responsibility for Print Preservation," *Ithaka S+R*, July 8, 2015, https://doi.org/10.18665/sr.241080.

funded, were therefore far less available to the general public. A great number of scientific journals were published by commercial organizations, making it difficult for small libraries to justify the subscription costs. The National Library of Medicine nearly uniquely pioneered efforts to ensure that the general public had free access to the journal literature that grew out of government-funded research.

Expanded Access

The early 2000s featured a number of library-led efforts to unlock access to collections and holdings, several of which were profiled in chapter 2. These efforts were largely about improving discovery of and access to cultural and intellectual heritage represented in the vast long tail of publications and special collections materials held by research libraries. Another strand of work focused on providing access to the recent scientific literature, which was already being published natively in digital format. All these efforts worked to reposition individual research libraries and the sector as a whole away from simply collecting resources for the needs of its own scholars and students and toward a growing emphasis on public access to its offerings.

Although the movement to improve access to the scientific journal literature is not the subject of the present study, it developed in parallel with the work of the dreamers and the values that drove it informed the work of the research libraries that participated in the Google book digitization project. Open access, as the movement was called, had its roots in efforts to enable scientists to circulate preprints of their work to one another digitally. Eventually, it would result in efforts to reform the nature of the journal publication model away from a subscription basis requiring a payment to access the publication. A variety of new models were introduced, including efforts to secure payment from scientists or their universities that enabled publishers to provide global free access to articles.[2]

The National Library of Medicine (NLM) took bold steps to address the availability of medical literature to the broader public. NLM, having established itself as a leader in providing bibliographic information in the 1970s, had long provided abstracts and indexes to medical literature to regional medical centers across the country. To ensure the availability of medical resources to physicians and public health professionals everywhere, the NLM developed a tiered bibliographic system that allowed for borrowing materials first at the local level, going to the regional level if necessary, and finally going to NLM as the medical library of last resort. The focus, though, was clearly on providing access to medical professionals. With the advent of the Internet, more individuals started to query the National Library of Medicine for medical information. In 2002, NLM, after vigorous debate among the Board of Regents, determined that it had an obligation to provide information resources to the general public. Medline Plus was launched in 1998 in response to the need. In 2000, the National Library of Medicine introduced Pubmed Central, a free digital archive of full-text scholarly articles published by biomedical and life sciences journal publishers. Under the strong leadership of David Lipman, director of the National Center for Biotechnology Information, and

2. For one early source, see Ann Okeson and James O'Donnell, *Scholarly Journals at the Crossroads: A Subversive Proposal for Electronic Publishing* (Washington, DC: Association of Research Libraries, 1995). See also the historical notes here: https://open-access.net/en/information-on-open-access/history-of-the-open-access -movement.

Donald Lindberg, director of NLM, Pubmed Central began by encouraging publishers to voluntarily contribute articles that resulted from federally funded research grants but later moved to legislation that required depositing articles that had been produced with government funds into the archives.

Efforts to increase the share of the broader scholarly literature made available through open access are still ongoing at the time of this writing, and the implications on the major publishing incumbents as well as the variety of smaller publishing houses are still yet to be determined. Even so, the zeal with which academic librarians advocated open access was a continuing feature of the sector in this period. The result was a substantial increase in the share of new scientific research that was freely available online, albeit without a corresponding increase in the work to translate scientific and medical research into formats that could be both understood by and accessible to the layperson.

Mass digitization projects, including especially the Google book digitization project, had two major immediate impacts on expanding access. The first was that discovery of the long tail of materials it contained improved dramatically. As we will see in chapter 5, this also had a substantial benefit for scholars, but the improved discovery would make it possible for any Google web search to pull up results from millions of books published over the course of hundreds of years. This alone helped to reanimate many of these works in the research of millions of users.

Second, the Google book digitization project (along with the other work of the dreamers) would make millions of volumes of public domain materials—those whose copyright had expired—freely available to all users. Much as open access models would ensure a licensing regime enabling free public access, so Google's decision not to "gate" the public domain works whose digitization it funded would improve access. Over time, this decision would prod other digitization initiatives with access provided on a subscription model to increase public access to the public domain materials in their collections.

Public Enthusiasm

In a 2004 interview for the *New York Times*, Paul Duguid, information scientist at the University of California, Berkeley, speculated that the Google digitization project that had been recently announced would "'blast wideopen' the walls around the libraries of world-class institutions."[3] It was a telling metaphor, one that suggested the belief that a vast public would find value if only those walls could finally come down.

The *New York Times* Sunday magazine of May 14, 2006, looked at the implications of Google for books, reading, and libraries in an extensive article by Kevin Kelly, a "senior maverick" of *Wired* magazine. Kelly observed that the digital library would be the 32 million books, 750 million articles and essays, 25 million songs, 500 million mages, 3 million videos and short films, and 100 billion public web pages—all of which could be compressed onto 50 petabyte technology. All of the recorded information would be available to anyone with a screen for digital reading.

Bill McCoy, the general manager of Adobe's e-publishing business, says: ". . . The most dramatic effect of digital libraries will be not on us, the well-booked, but on the billions of people worldwide who are underserved by ordinary paper

3. Felicia R. Lee, "Questions and Praise for Google Web Library," *New York Times*, December 18, 2004, https://www.nytimes.com/2004/12/18/books/questions-and-praise-for-google-web-library.html.

books." It is these underbooked—students in Mali, scientists in Kazakhstan, elderly people in Peru—whose lives will be transformed when even the simplest unadorned version of the universal library is placed in their hands.[4]

Kelly's notion of book digitization being in the public good mirrored the ideals of Brewster Kahle, who had been making the rounds to research libraries, trying to convince them that it was vitally important to digitize the world's knowledge and place it in the hands of the next generation. In December 2007, Kahle gave a TED Talk in which he argued that "universal access to all knowledge is in our grasp."[5] He boldly calculated that for the cost of a house (or garage in California)—$60,000—the world could have access to the 26 terabytes that would contain the 26 million books housed in the Library of Congress. He stressed the importance of remembering the slogan chiseled into the archway of the Boston Public Library—"Free to All"—as the digital library was constructed. Kahle argued that the copyright laws, especially when thinking about orphan works, need not apply to the construction of a universal digital library.

When David Balto, a Senior Fellow at the Center for American Progress Action Fund, testified before the House Judiciary Committee in September 2009, he emphasized the benefits of the Google project:

The Internet is a great device for creating new markets, democratizing knowledge, and increasing competition. Google Books takes full advantage of this opportunity to

---

4. Kevin Kelly, "Scan This Book!" *New York Times*, May 14, 2006, https://www.nytimes.com/2006/05/14/magazine/14publishing.html.

5. https://www.Ted.com/talks/brewster_kahle_builds_a_free_digital_library/transcript.

expand the world's access to knowledge. Anyone can simply go on the web and, through Google Books, reach an almost endless array of information on nearly any topic. At the start of the 20th century, Andrew Carnegie spent an enormous sum to build the first truly public libraries in this country—before then, our libraries were for the most part only available to the educated and affluent. Google has taken on tremendous risk and expense to perform a comparable service, one that creates a virtual library of unprecedented proportions to millions of people, regardless of location, economic status, or resources. Thanks to the Google Books project, any individual anywhere in the United States will have access to an unprecedented corpus of information.[6]

Joining the United States Students Association, the American Association of People with Disabilities, the League of United Latin American Citizens, the Leadership Conference on Civil Rights, and the National Federation of the Blind, Balto argued that the Google project was the country's best hope for bridging the digital divide. He imagined a world in which the economically disadvantaged, the physically disabled, the students who attended community colleges rather than the elite research institutions, and minority communities without access to excellent public libraries would have the same access as those privileged to have access to the greatest libraries. The Google project would be the great leveler in America.

For the average individual, with access only to a public library, Google's book digitization project made available enormous

6. https://www.americanprogressaction.org/issues/economy/reports/2009/09/10/6623/competition-that-works-why-the-google-books-project-is-good-for-consumers-and-competitors/.

amounts of historical and genealogical information that would otherwise have remained inaccessible.[7] Examples from authors, science journalists, and others, who would not have had ready access through the research libraries, abounded.[8]

Diffuse Value

Sometimes, as the examples above indicate, Google's book digitization project had substantial benefits to identifiable members of the general public. These examples alone suggest the great value of unlocking access. But, in some ways, it is possible that these examples mask the far larger, but more diffuse, public benefits of book digitization.

Here, we refer to the billions of individuals who use the Internet every day to discover information. They conduct keyword searches, use social media applications, and are presented with advertisements, all of which have served as vectors for disinformation and politicization. Every time vetted knowledge is introduced into a result set, whether directly or because digitized book content appears in Wikipedia pages or other secondary sources, it stands to improve the results. How many times did the project create individually infinitesimal value in this way? How much more value could it have produced if the project had established a new business model for book dissemination?

7. Dorothy A. May, "Google Books: Far More than Just Books," *Public Libraries Online*, October 20, 2015, http://publiclibrariesonline.org/2015/10/far-more-than-just-books/.

8. Carrie Russell, "5 Examples of the Value of Google Books' Search Function," *American Libraries*, December 2, 2015, https://americanlibrariesmagazine.org/blogs/e-content/5-examples-of-the-value-of-google-books-search-function/.

5

The Academy Protests

While the diffuse impacts of the book digitization project on the general public were important even if not always easy to quantify, the academy tended to focus much more on its own needs and concerns than on the benefits of taking down the walls that had surrounded its knowledge repositories. In this moment of possibility, the academy and its allies were not universally supportive. Without any question, some were jealous of the ability of a commercial enterprise to take such a bold step toward universal access. Others were concerned about the displacement of libraries and librarians. But many also feared the prospect of a single major corporate entity gaining outsized influence over the digital future of society's shared intellectual and cultural heritage. The academic community's concerns were not only rhetorical. Several library-led groups launched projects that offered alternatives. None of these alternatives, however, would displace the singular impact of the Google book digitization project.

Broad Reactions

Opinions of the Google digitization project varied widely, but there was no shortage of commentary about the advantages or disadvantages of Google's efforts.[1] Some librarians believed the Google project was the next phase of librarianship. Some saw the project as a direct threat to the profession. Many raised concerns about ceding library authority to a commercial organization, often citing digitization quality and cultural imperialism as reasons for worry.[2]

For librarians who had long dreamed of a modern-day, comprehensive, and universal equivalent of the Library of Alexandria, the Google announcement was encouraging. Google, in its announcement of library partnerships, invoked the dream of making all known knowledge accessible.

EXCITEMENT

For scholars, the reactions were largely positive but not without concerns. At Michigan, Courant recalls that the "general faculty reaction was overwhelmingly positive."[3]

Google tried to please both libraries and publishers by linking digitized text to physical locations where the books could be purchased from the publisher or consulted in a library. Librarians took pleasure in Google's decision to add a "Find it in a library" link on the Google Book Search page, although they

1. From 2005 to 2011, Charles W. Bailey maintained a comprehensive website of publications related to the Google digitization project. See Charles W. Bailey Jr., *Google Books Bibliography* (Houston: Digital Scholarship, 2005–11).

2. Jeffrey R. Young, "From Gutenberg to Google: Five Views on the Search-Engine Company's Project to Digitize Library Books," *Chronicle of Higher Education*, June 3, 2005, A24.

3. Courant, interview.

found it troubling when they learned that the link had been applied only to public domain material. It became increasingly clear that Google was still thinking about the business model for Google Book Search. On the one hand, Google was trying to please publishers; on the other hand, it was trying to satisfy librarians. Librarians would feel most comfortable if Google adopted their standard practices and procedures; publishers would be more comfortable if Google did nothing to threaten their sales and revenue. It was a fine line to walk.

JEALOUSY

The founding partners were pleased to be innovators in the library community. They were taking a risk in forging a partnership with Google, but they believed that it was a worthy risk. Without having to find grant funds or secure institutional funds to underwrite the creation of a digital library, a corporate partner would provide the large cash investment. But Google's announced partnership with five prestigious libraries also sent shock waves through the library community, and it left smaller innovators wondering how their digitization programs would fare against a large corporate initiative. For the library community as a whole, two issues dominated the conversation: Why these five institutions? And why were these negotiations carried out in secret?

Perhaps because the Google book digitization project initially involved only five large research libraries, other librarians from peer institutions were sharply divided on how enthusiastic they should be about Google's plan to create a universal library. Leaders of several libraries that are typically seen as peers of the initial five but which Google had not approached had a curious reaction. They felt that their collections were just as strong and their willingness to participate was no less great, and they certainly did not want their provosts or alumni to think that their libraries were somehow behind the times. Pride and jealousy were important emotions for those that were not invited initially. Did they also play a role in those that were in the elect? Mark Sandler recalls, "At the time, there was a great deal of jealousy about the Google Five and the handful of other schools that had been approached. Others thought it would be a real PR coup to be in that class of schools."[4] Donald Waters recalls, "There were some pretty nasty reactions from other libraries. There was no effort [by Google] to mollify that. In fact, they used that jealousy to pick off other libraries later."[5] For others, it was the secrecy that prompted sharp criticism. Libraries take pride in their openness and transparency. Why would leaders in the profession agree to sign contracts with firm nondisclosure clauses? Why had these plans not been brought to the attention of peers for discussion? The collaboration that research libraries had experienced in working on large-scale problems such as cataloging and preservation did not appear to stand up to the challenges of the digital age.

ANTI-COMMERCIALISM

One consistent theme among the librarians who worked in U.S. nonprofit higher education institutions was anti-commercialism. Michael Keller recalls that "several librarians began to object because Google is a commercial enterprise.

4. Deanna Marcum and Roger C. Schonfeld, interview with Mark Sandler, December 22, 2016.

5. Deanna Marcum and Roger C. Schonfeld, interview with Donald J. Waters, May 16, 2017.

My response was 'nonsense!' Google has digital images of our collections because of agreements we have made with them, but we have not made exclusive deals."[6]

The Google project was on every conference agenda and came up in practically every discussion among librarians in those early years. Librarians quickly realized that the commercial search engine provided something that traditional libraries could not match: speed and convenience. At the Public Library Association (PLA) conference in Boston on March 23, 2006, Ben Bunnell, a librarian on the Google Book Search team, announced that as of the day before 24,000 people had signed up for Google's librarian newsletter. All librarians attending the PLA meeting understood the power of such a large number. Some of the participants acknowledged that they were using Google Book Search to answer reference questions, but others complained that the results of such searches did not come back in subject subdivisions that librarians are accustomed to.[7]

QUALITY CONCERNS

Two of the major substantive concerns were the quality of the scans and the implications for existing library collections. On the one hand the scans must be high quality, but on the other hand the universities must be committed to sustaining the massive tangible collections even once digitized versions were made available.

Courant recalls the latter concern clearly. "There was an immediate concern from some departments that we would be

6. Keller, interview.
7. Andrew Albanese and Norman Oder, "Google Gains with Librarians: Newsletter Sign-ups Boom; Book Sales Launch; Where's Library Link?" *Library Journal*, April 15, 2006, p. 16.

destroying the physical collection. We assured them that the digital copy would be the use copy, but faculty would still have full rights to the printed copy. We said, you can get it somehow. We were not going to diminish in any way the physical collection."[8]

Over time, several academic studies examined the quality of the digitized output with some care and even if the volume was impressive found the quality to be wanting. Paul Duguid examined the quality of scanning in the famous literary work *Tristram Shandy*, showing an array of problems in the digitization.[9] Later, Paul Conway would conduct more systematic research of the underlying digitized corpus, along with a framework for assessing imperfections.[10] Over time, Google would undertake a variety of work to improve the quality of its scans and OCR.

Librarians and archivists were concerned about the implications for human labor, in particular the devaluing of expertise in selection and support. Librarians worried that students would continue to need their advice about how to navigate the large number of results from a search and to establish the validity and quality of those results.[11] Despite librarians' worries about possible inadequacies of Google, the public embraced the ease

---

8. Courant, interview.

9. Paul Duguid, "Inheritance and Loss? A Brief Survey of Google Books," *First Monday* 12, no. 8 (August 6, 2007), http://dx.doi.org/10.5210/fm.v12i8.1972.

10. P. Conway, "Archival Quality and Long-Term Preservation: A Research Framework for Validating the Usefulness of Digital Surrogates," *Archival Science* 11, no. 3 (2011): 293–309; P. Conway, "Measuring Content Quality in a Preservation Repository: HathiTrust and Large-Scale Book Digitization," Proceedings of 7th International Conference on Preservation of Digital Objects (iPres 2010), September 19–24, 2010, Vienna, Austria, pp. 95–102, http://hdl.handle.net/2027.42/85227; Paul Conway, "Preserving Imperfection: Assessing the Incidence of Digital Imaging Error in HathiTrust," *Digital Technology & Culture* 42, no. 1 (2013): 17–30, DOI 10.1515/pdtc-2013-0003.

11. Lee, "Questions and Praise for Google Web Library."

of finding digital information and greeted the book digitization project enthusiastically.[12]

CULTURAL IMPERIALISM

Concern about the Google partnership was not limited to the United States. On the international level, questions arose about how representative or comprehensive the Google book digitization project would be if the corporation worked exclusively with English-speaking institutions. National pride was also a factor. Why should the United States be the creator of a comprehensive digital library without the participation of major libraries in other countries?

The French press began writing with some concern that only libraries in English-speaking countries had been included among the founding partners in the Google book digitization project. The journalists did not realize (or recognize) that the large research libraries that had been included held books in hundreds of languages, not just English. President of France Jacques Chirac wrote to his counterparts in Germany, Hungary, Poland, and Spain in April 2005, urging them to join in an effort to create a digital European Library as a way to ensure that European cultures would not be sidelined by Google.[13] President Chirac proposed that the development of this digital library should become a goal of the European Commission

12. Edward J. Valauskas, "Googlization of Libraries: Debunking the Internet Godzilla Myth" (The Second Follett Lecture, Graduate School of Library and Information Science, Dominican University, February 15, 2006), http://worldlibraries.dom .edu/index.php/worldlib/article/view/91/28.

13. "Timeline of digitisation and online accessibility of cultural heritage" (July 23, 2014). European Commission, Digital Agenda for Europe. The letter, written in French, was dated April 28, 2005.

and encouraged the several European governments to agree to fund the effort.

Even as this was taking place, Google was negotiating to broaden its digitization efforts globally. Within a year of its first announcement, it had concluded agreements to expand its scanning efforts to eight sites in continental Europe.[14]

Fortunately for Europeana (the European Digital Library), Jean-Noël Jeanneney was the president of the Bibliothèque nationale de France from 2002 until 2007, where he was able to advance the cause of preserving European culture. As a historian of the media, he was able to press the case in international newspapers, calling attention to the arrogance and misguided judgment of a gigantic American corporation.[15] Jeanneney had an ally in the president of the European Commission. For more than a decade, the EU's Telematics for Libraries program had been working toward a digital library of European cultural heritage. The European Commission provided initial funding for the European Digital Library Network, the prototype for Europeana.

The French, in particular, were concerned with the homogenization of world culture, and Europeana was meant to be a parallel database of non-English-language materials. Richard Leiter notes that the French reaction was "a supreme irony about the Google project, and it was a result of a fundamental misunderstanding."[16] The European reaction was based on a

14. Edward Wyatt, "Google Opens 8 Sites in Europe, Widening Its Book Search Effort," *New York Times*, October 18, 2005, http://www.nytimes.com/2005/10/18/technology/google-opens-8-sites-in-europe-widening-its-book-search-effort.html.

15. Jeanneney, *Google and the Myth of Universal Knowledge*.

16. Richard A. Leiter, "Dodging and Weaving through the Online Libraries: Focus on Google Print," *Legal Information Alert* 24, no. 8 (September 1, 2005): 72.

belief that the Google book digitization project foretold the inevitable demise of physical libraries. In fact, Google had broad ambitions to offer many options, including providing readers new means of access to libraries and bookstores. Google's results page would provide links to bookstores, including Amazon.com and BarnesandNoble.com. It would also show the locations of nearby libraries where the reader could find the physical book.

The Andrew W. Mellon Foundation

The specter of a massive corporate project rallied librarians to consider other options. Individual libraries, even a consortium of institutions, could not match the financial resources Google brought to the book digitization project, but the philanthropic community could have been a counterforce, and the Andrew W. Mellon Foundation, with its long history of supporting the research needs of scholars, was the most likely to come to the rescue.

In May 2004, Michigan's John Wilkin wrote to Don Waters of the Mellon Foundation and Kevin Guthrie of ITHAKA to describe a "cooperative repository concept."[17] Mellon was at the time a foremost funder of selective higher education institutions, with special emphases on the humanities and libraries. ITHAKA was a not-for-profit organization that the Mellon, Hewlett, and Niarchos foundations had recently established to drive digital initiatives for higher education. At the time, Mellon and ITHAKA were tightly connected, including at the trustee level, and so in his thinking, Wilkin was looking to

---

17. Wilkin, memorandum.

Mellon for funding and to ITHAKA as an operational partner or governance vehicle.[18]

Wilkin approached Mellon and ITHAKA to request funding to support a repository of the files already being digitized by Google in the lead-up to the public announcement. As we will describe in greater detail in chapter 6, Wilkin envisioned a collective repository shared by all the partner libraries, allowing them to dramatically transform their approach to print collections and even library services more broadly. He requested funding to support the disk space initially to be housed at Michigan where the digitized files would be stored, as well as some additional funding to develop a collaborative governance structure.[19]

But the discussion did not proceed as Wilkin had hoped. This outreach from Michigan was the first clear word that Mellon received about Google's digitization plans, and at least in his advance memorandum Wilkin had intimated that "Google is in negotiation with a number of publishers to provide full viewing access to their in-copyright materials. They report a number of significant successes." Whether opening up access to vast amounts of publisher content was a possibility then being considered behind the scenes, or whether he had confused the publisher project with the library project, it appears that the prospect of Google building a full-access digital library set off alarm bells. Mellon and ITHAKA leaders, with their experience building JSTOR (of which Guthrie was then president) and other digital services for higher education, were not certain that a collaboration model involving Google and in-copyright

18. Marcum and Schonfeld are employees of ITHAKA at the time of publication, and Schonfeld was previously an employee of the Andrew W. Mellon Foundation.
19. Wilkin, memorandum.

materials was in the interest of the higher education community over the long term. Moreover, they must have wondered how it would position JSTOR over time as well.

Wilkin recalls a face-to-face discussion with Waters, Guthrie, and Mellon's then-president, William G. Bowen. He recalls Guthrie offering that public domain material could be added to JSTOR. But given the experience seeking permissions from copyright holders, and the need to compensate them commensurately, he recalls being advised to "steer clear of the in-copyright materials."[20]

The discussion came to a close without any agreement that Mellon would fund the initiative. Waters came away with the perspective that, although Wilkin's proposal was gesturing toward collaboration, "Michigan really wanted the help for itself."[21] And Mellon and ITHAKA leaders left the discussion determined to figure out what Google was up to and what it meant for their initiatives and the community more broadly.

Guthrie and Bowen spent a portion of that summer and fall trying to determine the best position to take on the Google digitization partnership. In July, Guthrie traveled to Silicon Valley to meet with Google staff to discuss shared interests. In his notes reflecting on what he learned, he was clearly surprised at how inexpensive Google had come to see storage and how prolific and non-selective it was prepared to be in being willing to store anything, no matter how small the potential audience. He also tried to establish whether Google was planning to sell content itself (like a database service such as JSTOR or a bookstore such as Amazon) or whether it was truly digitizing these

---

20. Wilkin, interview.
21. Waters, interview.

materials simply to provide free access or to be able to point elsewhere to access them.[22]

Discussions continued into the fall leading up to the December announcement, and it is clear that Mellon and ITHAKA were uncomfortable. Following trustee-level discussion about how to proceed, Mellon tried to see if it could marshal a group of libraries toward a different vision of collaboration, convening a meeting that included leaders and legal staff of the five libraries as well as ITHAKA.

The invitation letter from Bowen indicated that the meeting's purpose was "to engage in a highly confidential, open-ended brainstorming session about the interests involved and issues raised by mass digitization of scholarly content, and the potential benefits of coordinating the ways in which libraries respond to new opportunities," promising that the "discussion will focus on the broad strategic questions associated with mass digitization, not on any specific projects that may be contemplated or even underway." Mellon's unstated objective for this conclave would be to see if it could make an investment of sufficient scale such that book digitization would take place from within the research library community rather than through an initiative coordinated by a technology company.[23]

Reflecting on the meeting, Waters recalls, "It was very strange. They all agreed to come. But they sat around the table and couldn't say anything because of nondisclosure agreements and were afraid of damaging their relationship with Google. They wouldn't speak about the nature of their agreements. They were all making their own deals, and nothing could be done

---

22. Kevin Guthrie, "Confidential Memorandum: Meeting with Google Staff," July 28, 2004 (shared with authors).

23. William G. Bowen to William A. Gosling, September 22, 2014, HathiTrust files.

about any of it."[24] Wilkin recalls that generally at this stage "the nondisclosure piece hampered conversations with other institutions."[25]

In early November, Bowen and Guthrie together met with Eric Schmidt, Google's CEO at the time. Reflecting on that very candid conversation with some of the concern that he seemed to feel, Guthrie would write to Bowen, "Even if Michigan were not already signed up, and if we were to conclude that what Google is doing is not in the scholarly community's interest (a case that seems basically impossible to make at this stage) Mellon and Hewlett [which may also have been involved in preliminary conversations about an intervention] would have to expend enormous political capital to prevent it. This does not seem advisable, even if it is possible."[26]

The nature of this engagement with Google was not what Michigan was seeking when Wilkin approached Mellon and ITHAKA. Instead of funding to support a digital repository, whose eventual development will be chronicled in chapter 7, there was a sustained examination of the Google digitization initiative and its implications, not least for JSTOR, as well as some tentative efforts to explore an alternative.

Kevin Guthrie, in a 2019 conversation reflecting on what Mellon might have done in 2004–5, recalled that November meeting he and Bill Bowen had with Eric Schmidt. Bowen had approached Google with confidence, since Schmidt had been one of Bowen's economics students at Princeton. Bowen thought he would be able to convince Schmidt to work more

24. Waters, interview.
25. Wilkin, interview.
26. Kevin Guthrie to Bill Bowen, Confidential Memorandum: Draft, [November 12, 2014] (shared with authors).

openly and transparently with the research library community as he rolled out his plans, but during that meeting, it became painfully evident that Bowen realized that Mellon's $2.5 billion endowment paled in comparison to Google's $3 billion in annual revenue. Bowen, the most influential leader in the academic sector who was deeply committed to using technology for educational gain, simply did not have the firepower to compete. Mellon did not have adequate resources to be an influential partner, and Bowen backed away from his efforts to enlist Google in a partnership that would be more transparent and supported by the academy. Mellon decided to move on with its own agenda and focus on what it could accomplish with its endowment.[27]

Waters recalls: "We had already made our major investment in JSTOR. At the time, the big deal was ArtStor: primary sources were our main interest. Not the secondary materials. We had fairly big plans on the digitization of these visual materials. In the end we spent something like $42 million. I don't think there was really much room for us to do more with other kinds of formats or materials."[28] Ultimately, the Mellon Foundation did not attempt to fund massive library-based digitization projects. Instead, it turned to a close examination of the needs of scholars, focusing on a specific discipline's transformation, investing heavily in the development of resources and tools for ancient Near Eastern and classical studies, archaeology, medieval studies, early modern studies, and musicology.

Reflecting several years later on some criticisms that the Google partnership would receive, Paul Courant nearly named Mellon in explaining that Google was the only feasible partner:

27. Deanna Marcum, interview with Kevin Guthrie, August 20, 2019.
28. Waters, interview.

"Would I prefer that a charitable foundation would support this work on the same schedule as Google, and make everything available to everyone, subject only to copyright restrictions? You bet. I would prefer it even more if that foundation would buy out all of the rights holders for all out-of-print works. Can someone tell me the name of the foundation, please? In the meantime, it seems to me that being in bed with Google is better than sleeping alone."[29]

The Open Content Alliance

Google's large footprint did not discourage everyone. Indeed it energized others. Brewster Kahle continued to lobby for an alternative to Google. Perhaps it was because of his deep knowledge of the technology sector that Kahle was quick to point out the dangers of relying on a corporate entity to achieve a social good.

Kahle, a strong advocate of open access, had contacted Google when he first learned that book digitization was of interest. He saw the Internet Archive as a vehicle for creating a universal digital library, and the appeal of working with Google was seductive. He arranged to give a presentation at Google's offices on his notion of a universal digital library and was delighted that both Sergey Brin and Eric Schmidt were in the audience.[30] Brin suggested that Google and Internet Archive combine forces to make book digitization a single project.

Upon further discussion, however, Kahle realized that Google had in mind something that was too commercial for

29. Paul Courant, "On Being in Bed with Google," November 4, 2007, http://paulcourant.net/2007/11/04/on-being-in-bed-with-google/.
30. Kahle, interview.

his taste. Google would pay for the digitization, but its eventual business plan (discussed in chapter 6) involved charging a subscription fee for access to the complete collection. This plan struck Kahle as "overly corporate."

Instead, Kahle began looking for support to develop a competing digitization effort at a similar scale to the Google book digitization project. In a first step, Kahle called Jesse Ausubel at the Sloan Foundation and pleaded for help in "fighting the war" against a corporate model. He argued that what is in the public domain must stay in the public domain, and Ausubel agreed to offer financial support for creating a freely accessible, universal digital library.[31]

Kahle understood that he needed buy-in from libraries to realize his dream, and he went to work to identify partners in what he would call the Open Content Alliance, announced publicly in October 2005. Yahoo, a direct competitor of Google's, along with the Internet Archive, the University of Toronto, the University of California, and the UK National Archives, banded together to form the alliance, which aimed to digitize hundreds of thousands of books over the next several years.[32] In contrast to Google, the Open Content Alliance pledged to make its digitized content available to any search engine, including Google. The alliance also sidestepped copyright entanglements by working only with public domain materials. Hewlett Packard and Adobe Systems donated equipment and the Internet Archive took responsibility for the actual scanning. Yahoo contributed cash, as did the University of California. Brewster Kahle

31. Ibid.

32. Katie Hafner, "In Challenge to Google, Yahoo Will Scan Books," *New York Times*, October 3, 2005, https://www.nytimes.com/2005/10/03/business/in-challenge-to-google-yahoo-will-scan-books.html.

called on other corporate and cultural organizations—even Google—to join this effort to create a universal digital library. Daniel Greenstein, director of the California Digital Library (CDL), observed that this open platform that made content widely available was the solution librarians had been seeking.

Shortly after the launch of the Open Content Alliance, Microsoft announced that it would also join the project that was in competition with Google. Microsoft took an additional step of making its scanned content available through MSN, its portal service, through which it would make "value added presentations of complete book information" at a fee. Microsoft clearly saw an advantage of linking book content to its web search offerings. Google was gaining dominance, and Microsoft wanted to impede Google's progress. At the outset, Microsoft relied on the Internet Archive to scan the public domain books offered for scanning by libraries, but the plan was to partner with copyright owners directly to gain permission to make the content available through the MSN portal.

The founders of the Open Content Alliance believed that librarians, who had expressed so much concern about the Google project and about the dangers of working with corporate interests, would quickly join this open, transparent initiative. Librarians critical of the project charged that Microsoft was not that different from Google. Not all thought Kahle's motives were entirely selfless; others bristled when Kahle referred to himself as a librarian rather than a technologist.

Despite strong efforts to involve more libraries in the Open Content Alliance, Kahle convinced only one to provide full-throated support. Carole Moore, then university librarian at the University of Toronto, committed to scan all of its public domain books and allowed the Open Content Alliance to set up a scanning hub on-site. Before Moore retired in 2011, all of the out-of-copyright books in the library's collection had been scanned.

In the end, the project did not scale nearly as large as that of its Google competitor. In all likelihood, the project stalled because librarians simply had mixed views about the best way to proceed. Should they join a not-for-profit collaboration? Should they embrace Google's vision? Should they lobby the Library of Congress to be more inclusive? Should they seek more donor assistance so they could proceed individually? The answer was not clear.

The Open Content Alliance moved ahead haltingly, and over the next three years Microsoft had scanned and indexed 750,000 volumes from libraries. But in May 2008, Microsoft withdrew from the project. Satya Nadella, senior vice president of search, portal, and advertising, issued a blog post that cited the reason for cessation of the project: "Based on our experience, we foresee that the best way for a search engine to make book content available will be by crawling content repositories created by book publishers and libraries."[33]

Harvard's Proposed DPLA

Robert Darnton voiced grave concerns about the implications of the knowledge found in libraries being bound up in a corporate environment. Darnton arrived at Harvard in July 2007 to take up responsibilities as the university's librarian. Having been a professor of book history at Princeton for most of his career, he had not had dealings with Google or its book project, but on his first day in his new office, one of the university

---

33. Mac Slocum, "Microsoft Closing Live Search Books," May 23, 2008, http://toc .oreilly.com/2008/05/microsoft-shuttering-live-sear.html.

attorneys met with him to explain Harvard's involvement in the Google book digitization project and to describe the confidential negotiations under way with the Authors Guild and the Association of American Publishers to reach a settlement. Darnton participated in some of Google's settlement discussions, until "it eventually became clear to me that they were planning to convert Google's original search service, which I considered a good idea, into a commercial library, which I thought was a terrible idea."[34]

Michigan, Stanford, and the University of California had permitted Google to digitize books from their collections that were covered by copyright, but Harvard, on advice from legal counsel, had not. Darnton, who went into considerable detail about his interest in opening up Harvard's collections as a public good, could not agree to infringing copyright law. He explained that "all research libraries were tempted by the possibility of having their holdings digitized free of charge, and many librarians hoped the settlement could be framed in a way that benefited the general public." Instead, in his view, Google elected to sweep copyright aside, via a class-action strategy, to create a commercial library, that is, "to charge libraries for our own books, in digital form, for a price that could spiral out of control as badly as the prices of academic journals."[35]

For a while, when Robert Darnton was actively pushing the idea, it seemed that the Digital Public Library of America (DPLA) might become a comprehensive digital library. Darnton's passion for making the deep and rich collections of Harvard and other major research libraries available almost made the ideal seem possible. His eloquent writing captured

34. Deanna Marcum, interview with Robert Darnton, August 6, 2018.
35. Ibid.

the imagination of academics and some foundations. Darnton's inspired contribution was that he included public libraries in the earliest conversations about DPLA. He worked collaboratively with John Palfrey (then Harvard's law librarian) to seek support from government agencies such as the Institute of Museum and Library Services and the National Endowment for the Humanities, which were persuaded to invest financial resources that allowed small libraries, museums, and historical societies to become part of the dream. Regional digitization hubs, funded by grants, made it possible for these small institutions to contribute their specialized holdings to DPLA. It looked as if an egalitarian digital library could be created. The more difficult aspect of Darnton's vision of DPLA is that he talked about it in terms of being a free resource. Assuming that foundations and government agencies would find the idea so compelling that they would pay for access for all, Darnton did not build a business model for DPLA, and since foundations and government granting agencies alike are inclined to pay for start-ups but not ongoing operations, subsequent leaders of DPLA found it difficult to deliver on the promise of free access. In 2012, Palfrey left Harvard to become the head of school at Phillips Academy, and from 2012 to 2015 he also served as the founding president of the Board of Directors of DPLA. In May 2013, DPLA announced that Dan Cohen, a tenured professor in the Department of History and Art History at George Mason University and the director of the Roy Rosenzweig Center for History and New Media, would be the founding executive director of DPLA. Despite the heroic efforts of Palfrey and Cohen, with their extensive knowledge and contacts in the philanthropic world, a financial model for a comprehensive digital library that would be freely available to the public remained elusive. Palfrey went on to become the president of the MacArthur Foundation in 2019, while Cohen moved to Northeastern University as dean of libraries and vice provost for information collaboration in 2017. The mission and aspirations of DPLA changed dramatically over the years, and by 2019 it sought grants from foundations to develop better e-book readers, a far cry from its original purpose.[36]

No Match for Google

These efforts to identify alternatives generated real advances in digital library development, even though no single alternative matched Google's project. Over time, research libraries either used their own funds or secured grant funding to digitize portions of their collections and in the process converted their staffs to digital librarians. Without coordination, these efforts proved to be locally useful in that staff learned how to digitize materials and manage digital collections. They developed digital services that garnered attention from the rest of the academic community as they made their intentions clear about embracing the digital world. But these digital projects were added to local websites and the content was buried several layers down, making it next to impossible for scholars and students to find it.

While public-minded Brewster Kahle wanted to inspire a non-commercial digitization movement and several research libraries thought it would be good to take responsibility themselves for creating digital libraries, all of these efforts simply could not compete with the Google initiative. Too much money

---

36. In a twist, DPLA would later partner with Amazon Publishing to distribute its e-book. https://dp.la/news/dpla-signs-agreement-with-amazon-publishing-to-make-their-ebooks-available-to-u-s-libraries.

was required—money that the libraries did not have. More than that, possibly, was the difficulty that individual institutions had in joining forces with their colleagues to take on a large, complex project.

A great many librarians, and some scholars who followed the Google project closely, wished for a collaborative, noncommercial, comprehensive digital library. The research library community, in particular, urged the Library of Congress to assume a national leadership role that would lead to a decentralized, inclusive digital library that would be supported by federal funds and made freely accessible to the public. Technical infrastructure alone may have kept this dream from being realized, but more importantly, the Library of Congress had launched a highly successful fund-raising campaign through the creation of the James Madison Council. Securing funds from donors in support of the Library of Congress (along with recognition from donors' elected officials) was easier than making a case for a loose collaboration of research libraries. The research library community hoped for national coordination and shared decision making. The Library of Congress hoped to be recognized for its leadership in providing primary source materials to the elementary and secondary education community.

Brewster Kahle's initiatives had many of the right elements to satisfy the library community: collections would be open, any library could be part of the greater whole, and the technical infrastructure was in place. Yet, the question kept recurring, "What happens if Brewster isn't there?" The Internet Archive, a nonprofit organization, did not appear to have a viable future separate from its founder. An added complication was Kahle's lack of understanding of the library community's bibliographic practices or its practitioners' deliberative approach to solving problems. And in any event, while Kahle could style himself as a librarian, the library community was uneasy in its acceptance of an individual and an organization that remained outside their traditional boundaries. But the more serious challenge was that, even for all the successes of the Internet Archive and its digitization partnerships for generating content, these materials remained outside the mainstream Internet search environment, which Google increasingly came to control.

Individual philanthropies, though sympathetic to digital library development, were not prepared to invest the massive resources required, especially since the library community did not agree about the best approach.

While several well-intentioned plans were launched, it was difficult to challenge the market leader. Google alone not only had the financial resources, the commitment of its leaders, and the ability to move decisively and quickly but also increasingly controlled the discovery environment.

6

Publishers, Legal Issues, Settlement

While the public access benefits of Google's book digitization project were unquestioned, and the academy struggled with losing control of this valuable content, many publishers took an even dimmer view of the initiative. For them, what is allowable under copyright law was at the heart of the controversy. Google relied on the application of fair use in its digitization efforts. It took the position that digitizing print books was transformative, that is, it unlocked an array of digital value that was trapped in the print versions. Publishers saw themselves losing out on the value contained in their copyright assets. After years of tussle, a win-win outcome was nearly reached.

Copyright and Technological Advances

The notion that technological advances outpaced the copyright law was not new. When the photocopy machine became a staple in libraries, application of the copyright law became more confusing. Questions about photocopies and fair use came to a head in a legal case, *Williams and Wilkins Co. v. United States*. In 1973, medical publishers Williams and Wilkins sued the National Library of Medicine (NLM) and the National Institutes of Health. Having developed an automated index of the medical literature, the National Library of Medicine launched a new service for medical researchers. For those who were not in the Washington, D.C., area, it made photocopies of medical articles (some published by Williams and Wilkins) and sent them to those conducting medical research. NLM did not monitor the reason for the request, and researchers could keep the copies they received. The publisher claimed copyright infringement and sued. NLM argued that photocopying medical articles for researchers constituted fair use. The U.S. Court of Claims noted that a study of copyright was already under way and directed the continuation of NLM's practice during the interim. Judge James F. Davis determined that there had been no infringement, that the challenged use was "fair" in view of the combination of all the factors involved in consideration of "fair" or "unfair." The court noted that the plaintiff did not prove that its business had been significantly harmed by NLM's photocopying practices. The court was convinced that not providing the photocopies of medical articles would no doubt harm medicine and medical practice. Finally, the court held that balancing the interests of science and those of publishers would ultimately require a legislative solution.

The Williams and Wilkins case captured significant attention from the publishing community. They clearly understood that technology was moving faster than the copyright law, and publishers, librarians, and researchers pushed Congress to revisit the legislation.

In 1976, the revised copyright law extended the duration of protection to the life of the author plus fifty years. The earlier law provided protection for twenty-eight years, with the possibility of extending protection for another twenty-eight years. The 1976 revision was drafted in anticipation of the Berne Convention, and Congress felt it necessary to bring U.S. copyright law into alignment with international law. Another motivation for revising the law was to take into account the new media forms that had not been covered by earlier versions of copyright law. In response to the highly publicized Williams and Wilkins case, a new section was added, Section 108, that allowed library copying without permission for purposes of scholarship, preservation, and interlibrary loan under certain circumstances. Section 107, added at the same time, allowed for copyright exceptions, based on the application of four tests for fair use:

- the purpose and character of the use
- the nature of the copyrighted work
- the amount and substantiality of the portion taken
- the effect of the use upon the potential market

It was in the 1994 Supreme Court case *Campbell v. Acuff-Rose Music, Inc.* that the priority of the first factor in determining fair use was made clear. The most important question, the Court said, is whether the material has been used to help create something new or merely copied verbatim into another work. Has the material taken from the original work been transformed by adding new expression or meaning? Was value added to the original by creating new information, new aesthetics, new insights, and understandings?

Copyright law is a specialized field, full of advocates for the positions that are in their own best interests, and few understand all of its nuances in a balanced fashion. Digital technology opened up dizzying possibilities for creating and disseminating content. For many of the emerging technology companies, the copyright law seemed archaic, and Google seemed especially willing to discount its intricacies. Major research libraries were typically guided by their universities' legal counsel to avoid the risk of suits whenever possible. When Google's lawyers argued that scanning books was a fair use activity, some librarians applauded the company's bravery; others scorned its audacity. Publishers found little reason to celebrate. They were already struggling with lagging sales of monographs, and it would not help the bottom line to have more works being made freely available online. From their perspective, Google was violating their intellectual property rights. Legal counsel for Google firmly believed that book digitization could result in the expansion of copyright. For librarians and publishers alike, the legal questions could determine their future. But the legal implications also affected broad societal issues.

While librarians, publishers, and Google argued about how copyright law influenced book digitization policy, the general public focused on the benefits of a digital library. Journalist Kevin Kelly placed book digitization in the category of one of society's moral imperatives. He believed the dream of the universal library had been resurrected: "the explosive rise of the Web going from nothing to everything in a decade, has encouraged us to believe in the impossible again."[1]

To technologists, the book digitization project promised that technology would deliver a universal library. Kelly optimistically predicted:

---

1. Kelly, "Scan This Book!"

Whether this vast mountain of dark books is scanned by Google, the Library of Congress, the Chinese or by readers themselves, it will be scanned well before its legal status is resolved simply because technology makes it so easy to do and so valuable when done. In the clash between the conventions of the book and the protocols of the screen, the screen will prevail. On this screen, now visible to one billion people on earth, the technology of search will transform isolated books into the universal library of all human knowledge.[2]

But at whose expense? Publishers did not share this utopian view and took exception to Google's declaration of intent to digitize books without regard to copyright status. They argued that Google was overreaching by not securing permission from and providing payments to the publishers that held the copyright.

Reanimating Books

Librarians' and publishers' divergent views of copyright became apparent during the public hearings on the 1976 copyright legislation. When Google made it clear that it did not worry unduly about copyright barriers but focused, instead, on the public good, librarians saw an ally. Google had expected more support from publishers, believing that the longer period of copyright protection granted in 1976 only exacerbated their problems of storing copies of their books in warehouses for many years. In addition, Google believed that publishers would

2. Ibid.

support its plan to scan their inventories, which would open up a new revenue stream for them.

When Google launched its digitization initiative, the goal was to allow searching inside books. The books that were still copyright protected would not be available in their entirety; just snippets would be accessible. Google described this service as analogous to a card catalog. According to Google's general counsel David Drummond, scanning was protected by the fair use provision of the copyright law, much the same as a cataloging record. "'We are not creating a substitute for the work by scanning the full text of the work,'" he said in an interview with *Publishers Weekly*. "'We are creating an electronic card catalogue and to do that, you have to copy that whole thing.'"[3] Competitors and publishers themselves, however, saw opportunities to do far more with digitized books than create a discovery service with them. For them, the danger was that digitized texts could easily be copied and sent to others without going through the publisher, risking a significant loss of revenue.

Google was not the only company thinking about technological possibilities. Only two days after Google launched its Google Print project, which included only out-of-copyright books, Amazon introduced two new programs: Amazon Pages and Amazon Upgrade. Amazon attempted to do for books what Apple Computer's iTunes did for music. It would allow a consumer to buy an entire book, or just parts of it, much like consumers could buy a specific song without buying the entire album. Amazon Pages allowed the purchase of a chapter or

3. Jim Milliot, "Google: Library Program Is Fair Use," *Publishers Weekly*, October 7, 2005, https://www.publishersweekly.com/pw/print/20051010/29231-google-library-program-is-fair-use.html.

even a relevant page. With Amazon Upgrade the customer had online access to any book purchased.

Publishers also saw opportunities and took advantage of digital technology to offer new services. In November 2005, Random House announced that it planned to work with both Google and Yahoo to offer its books "à la carte" for small payments, perhaps as low as 99 cents for four pages of the book. Richard Sarnoff, president of Random House's Corporate Development Group at the time, noted, "'We believe that it is important for publishers to be innovative in providing digital options for consumers to access our content, especially in light of the emergence of ubiquitous Internet access and improved display technologies that can support sustained reading.'"[4]

On November 14, 2005, the *Wall Street Journal* announced that Google was having conversations with publishers about a plan to rent digital copies of books they had published. At about the same time, Microsoft announced that it would be working with the British Library to digitize its books, and Yahoo, in partnership with Brewster Kahle, formed the Open Content Alliance to create a digital archive of "globally sourced digital collections, including multimedia content."[5] The Open Content Alliance would include only digital versions of public domain content.

Some of these plans must have been appealing to publishers, who had fretted over their out-of-print books for years. When they did not sell all of the print copies of a title, the only option was to store them in a warehouse, waiting for customers

4. Elinor Mills, "Amazon, Random House Throw Book at Google," CNET, November 3, 2005, https://www.cnet.com/news/amazon-random-house-throw-book-at-google/.

5. "Will the Online Book Publishing Flap Rewrite the Copyright Law?" *Knowledge @ Wharton*, February 8, 2006.

to purchase them. Warehousing expenses significantly affected the publishers' profit margins. When legislators added to the length of protection for copyrighted works, more and more out-of-print books nevertheless remained in copyright, creating a class of books that were not being sold but were not in the public domain—a category of copyright limbo called "orphan works." Google's pitch to publishers was that digitizing orphan works would bring them "back into print"—at no expense to publishers. Google further argued that these books that had been in copyright limbo would now be readily discoverable in digital form. Google held out hope to the publishers that when users could find these "orphan works" through Google searches, they would want to purchase these titles. Even though publishers did not have an immediate business plan for charging for discoverability and demand, they were intrigued by the possibility of turning the liability of warehoused titles into an asset. Of course, the publishers expressed keen interest in this prospect of turning the cost of book storage into a profit center, even if the beneficiary of the new system was not entirely clear.

For Google and its competitors, determining the copyright status of individual books was not an easy task. The Copyright Office did not maintain a comprehensive list of the copyright status of out-of-print books, so it was extremely difficult to determine what could be legally digitized. Publishers maintained surprisingly uneven records of their intellectual property, probably because they were more concerned about selling their new books than about detailed inventory records. And given the complexity of the previous copyright regime, with optional renewals, it was exceedingly difficult to be certain whether many publications were even under copyright. With the status of approximately 75 percent of recorded texts being uncertain, neither publishers nor librarians had been willing to take the legal risk of investing large sums to digitize these materials.

Google was willing to take the risk. While librarians and publishers alike were more likely to ask what was allowed under copyright law, patiently biding their time for an opportunity to lobby to change it, Google thought the law was antiquated and not especially relevant in the digital age. Google determined that it would scan the full corpus of books, even the 75 percent that seemed too risky to everyone else. The company pledged to scan entire books, even when the copyright status was unclear, and use the scanned content to create a searchable index. The entire corpus could be searched, but only "snippets" (little different from catalog cards, Google argued) would be shown to the reader.

While publishers wrestled with how they could work with Google to scan their inventories of out-of-print books, Google realized that the largest inventories of these orphan works were found in research libraries. By working with libraries, Google did not have to deal with publishers who had incomplete inventories of the books they had published. Google did not at first recognize what librarians knew: library inventories and the metadata describing library collections were riddled with inconsistencies and mistakes. By working with five of the largest, most comprehensive libraries, Google projected producing a library of ten million scanned books. The scanned books would be indexed, but the search results would be rendered in different ways. Public domain works would be available in their entirety, with every page made available in full. For those books that were still in print, Google promised to work with publishers to determine what parts of their books would be accessible and under what conditions. For works for which it had no permission to display and which might still be under copyright, Google would show only "snippets." The copyright owner could opt out of participating at any time after establishing ownership of the copyright.

Publisher Doubts

Throughout the early period of the Google project, publishers thought they were having exclusive conversations with the company. It came as a surprise to many when they learned of Google's plans to digitize vast swathes of library collections. Publishers could not fathom how libraries could possibly secure permission for scanning books from so many publishers. As Dan Clancy remembers clearly, "publishers did not know about our library program" before it was announced.[6] After the announcement was made, several publishing industry leaders were quoted expressing tentative support or at least acquiescence at the point of the announcement. That support would prove to be brief.

At first, publishers were simply irritated. Perhaps most prominently, Patricia Schroeder, president of the Association of American Publishers at that time, said within days of the announcement, "At the moment, there are no alarm bells ringing from members. Many are consulting with Google. . . . We are ever vigilant, but unless the system crashes or we see large-scale piracy or leakage or changes in Google's business models, our people are being cooperative." Indeed, she specifically denied any expectation of legal action.[7]

Initially, publishers saw Google's snippet-view approach for in-copyright materials as substantively identical to Amazon's

---

6. Clancy, interview.
7. Quint, "Google and Research Libraries Launch Massive Digitization Project."

"look inside the book" feature, serving to improve discoverability, promotion, and potentially sales. David Steinberger, president and chief executive of the Perseus Books Group, spoke from this context to say, "I think there is minimal risk, or virtually no risk, of copyrighted material being misused."[8] Publishers began to talk with one another about Google's plans and sensed cause for alarm. Both the American Association of University Presses (AAUP; subsequently renamed the Association of University Presses) and the Association of American Publishers (AAP) were concerned about the library digitization program. In a letter dated May 20, 2005, Peter Givler, executive director of AAUP, asked Google for sixteen points of clarification about Google's book digitization initiative project, indicating that it "appears to involve systematic infringement of copyright on a massive scale."[9] Also citing copyright concerns, AAP first asked Google to suspend the book digitization project for six months. AAP's vice president for Legal and Governmental Affairs, Allan R. Adler, told the *Chronicle of Higher Education* that the group made the request in a June 10, 2005, letter that stopped short of calling for the project to "cease and desist." Adler insisted that they had simply asked for six months to take stock of what was happening, noting that Google had not provided satisfactory answers to the publishers' important questions. Google responded to both publishers' associations, believing it was only a matter of explaining better the advantages of the Google Print project. Adam Smith, the Google Print product manager, claimed in several newspaper interviews about the project that Google

8. Markoff and Wyatt, "Google Is Adding Major Libraries to Its Database."

9. "Publishers Question Google Print Library Project," *American Libraries*, August 1, 2005, p. 15 (2).

was completely in line with principles of fair use.[10] The publishers doubted that assertion.

The relationship with the Authors Guild proved to be more vexing. The Authors Guild supported any activity that brought more exposure for individual authors' works. The invocation of fair use for digitization was threatening, however. Google was surprised by the opposition of authors. From its perspective, scanning would help readers find authors they did not know about. It could widen the audience for members of the Authors Guild, especially the lesser-known ones, and provide a new stream of royalties.

The publishers were also concerned about the connection between the scanned books and the advertising that Google was selling. Richard Sarnoff, then chairman of the AAP board, noted that even if there would never be advertising on the pages displaying the books themselves, the books were an enormous draw of users to Google and an opportunity for them to be drawn to Google's revenue-producing properties: "Although there was no profit motivation in the [book search] activity, the overall economics of the Google model is why we thought it had a commercial element."[11] Clancy contends that book digitization was never an economic activity for Google. "I don't think this was great for the P&L—it was more that this was on mission."[12] But publishers were not convinced that Google's project was purely altruistic, and questions began to arise about whether the project should be seen to fall under fair use. Regardless of how the books were displayed and accessed,

10. Yuki Noguchi, "Google Delays Book Scanning," *Washington Post*, August 13, 2005, http://www.washingtonpost.com/wp-dyn/content/article/2005/08/12/AR2005081201694.html.

11. Sarnoff, interview.

12. Clancy, interview.

publishers became concerned that the very act of making a digital copy would, if permitted, shift the balance of fair use. Sarnoff's view is that "I don't think [Google] had really considered how publishers would have viewed the knock-on effects, with the slippery slope of how far can you push fair use."[13] Publishers had no interest in giving up rights under copyright by remaining passive.

More importantly, publishers feared that Google Print would deprive them of potential revenue. If readers could find digitized versions of books online, they had no incentive to purchase those books from the publishers. Google's defense was that the full content would be displayed only when the books were in the public domain, while for in-copyright materials it would display only "snippets" of books. Even though the full content of a book would not be made available, publishers worried that, for certain use cases, even search combined with snippet-level availability could cost them sales. And Google would be able to control any potential republishing of orphan works, creating a dilemma for publishers.[14]

Another concern was security: Google's digitized copies could be hacked or otherwise leak out, becoming publicly available. As Richard Sarnoff recalled, "We never really had a beef with the libraries because the libraries were never espousing that they would do anything intentionally with these files that we found untoward. They wanted to provide a certain amount of archival backup, which we were fine with, and a limited amount of access, which didn't concern us. The problem was

13. Sarnoff, interview.
14. Edward Wyatt, "Google Library Database Is Delayed," *New York Times*, August 13, 2005, https://www.nytimes.com/2005/08/13/books/google-library-database-is-delayed.html.

if the files got out of their hands."[15] There could also have been problems if the libraries used these files to test fair use boundaries of importance to them. Even though an increasing number of librarians spoke about the limitations of copyright law and many advocated "doing something," there was an overriding fear, especially among university legal counsels, of the associated liability of digitizing books and making them accessible online.

The publishers had little reason to distrust libraries, but they fully understood that the new technology made things that had been difficult in the print world incredibly easy. They had not yet experienced the campaign for open access or heard from the technologists who claimed that "information wants to be free." All of that would come later, but in the early years of the new millennium, publishers recognized that huge changes were coming, and they wanted to protect their industry as best they could.

The Legal Case: A Fork in the Road

Google was a bit naive about the extent to which copyright protections were critical to the publishers' business models. Google recognized that not all publishers would be willing to have their content be available online and had provided an "opt out" provision to address publishers' hesitation.[16] Asking publishers to opt their titles out, rather than accepting the burden of working with publishers to negotiate for which titles would be included, appears to have enraged the publishers. Schroeder

15. Sarnoff, interview.

16. Noguchi, "Google Delays Book Scanning"; *Los Angeles Times*, August 13, 2005, Saturday, Business Desk, Part C, pg. 1.

was adamant: "We think they have to stop this entirely. . . . This idea that the rights holder has all the burden . . . that's crazy."[17] The Authors Guild, along with a handful of individual authors, filed suit against Google in the United States District Court for the Southern District of New York on September 20, 2005. Five publishers—McGraw-Hill, Pearson, Penguin, Simon and Schuster, and John Wiley & Sons—sued Google in the same court one month later on October 19, 2005. Ultimately, the two cases were consolidated into a single action.[18] In this first suit, neither the Authors Guild nor the Association of American Publishers sued the partner libraries for offering their book collections to Google for scanning or for the digital copies Google was returning to them.

Ultimately, there were two major legal cases brought by the Authors Guild and/or the Association of American Publishers. A host of legal articles have examined the details and implications of these two suits, and a complete legal story can be found in Jonathan Band's exemplary work.[19]

The second lawsuit was initiated when the Authors Guild sued HathiTrust. As described in chapter 7, HathiTrust was formed in 2008, after the court rejected the proposed settlement. HathiTrust, operating under the auspices of the University of Michigan, initiated a partnership among major research libraries to collect the digital copies of books that had been

17. Notwithstanding the rising rhetoric on the library digitization work, publishers and Google remained partners on the publisher program and other forms of collaboration. "We were partners while they were suing us." Clancy, interview.

18. Case Management Order Regarding Coordination and Scheduling at 2–3, *Authors Guild v. Google, Inc.*, 05 Civ 8136 (DC) (S.D.N.Y. May 22, 2006).

19. For a complete description of the legal case, see Jonathan Band, "The Long and Winding Road to the Google Book Settlement," *John Marshall Review of Intellectual Property Law* 9, no. 2 (Winter 2009): 227–329.

scanned by Google and deposit them in a digital preservation repository located at the University of Michigan. HathiTrust proposed to amass digital copies of books that resulted from a number of initiatives, including the Google book digitization project, Internet Archive, Microsoft, and in-house scanning efforts of partner libraries.

What is most interesting in these two cases, we believe, is the apparent fork in the road that the legal issues represented. One path led toward settlement of the case that included monetization of the corpus and wide accessibility to a comprehensive digital library. The other path would shut down Google's ability to disseminate the books it was digitizing, leaving the job of creating a universal digital library to the existing book publisher and library ecosystem. Which path would be followed?

The Proposed Settlement

It is useful to review the proposed settlement again, if only to determine if there are parts of it that might still advance a digital library that is broadly useful to society. What is most interesting about the settlement is that all parties agreed to it without intervention. It took thirty months, but it was a winning solution for all involved.

The settlement would have served all parties' interests. Google would sell access to the publishers' copyrighted works, distributing a portion of the revenues to them. Universities and colleges would have the benefit of a database of digitized out-of-print books. Google would be able to offer a digital library.

The Authors Guild, by filing a class-action lawsuit, effectively involved every author and publisher with a book in an American library. In the proposed settlement, copyright owners would agree to release any claims against Google for scanning and making accessible their books. In return, the authors and publishers would enjoy a financial benefit. Jeff Cunard, a partner in the Debevoise & Plimpton law firm that represented the publishers, noted, "'If you have a kind of institutional problem, you can address the issue through a class-action settlement mechanism, which releases all past claims and develops a solution on an ongoing basis. And I think the genius here was of those who saw this as a way of addressing the problem of out-of-print books and liberating them from the dusty corners to which they had been consigned.'"[20]

The solution of a class-action suit, arguably, had more advantages for the little-known authors than the big-name authors. In this proposed settlement, publishers would be able to participate in a collective licensing regime for out-of-print books. Google would be able to display and sell the digital versions of these orphan books, but 63 percent of the revenue would go into escrow for the Book Rights Registry. The registry's funds would be distributed to rights holders as they came forward to claim their rights. In cases where ownership was not clear, registry funds would be used to sort out who actually owned the rights. The proposed settlement had the virtue of achieving the authors' and publishers' dreams of being paid something for their work *and* having their works read by larger audiences.

The proposed settlement would have resulted in Google taking financial responsibility for a one-time $45 million payout to the copyright holders of books it had scanned, $15.5 million in legal fees to publishers, $30 million to the authors, and $34.5 million for creating the Book Rights Registry—a total of $125 million.[21]

---

20. Somers, "Torching the Modern-Day Library of Alexandria."
21. Ibid.

The proposed settlement was as radical as it would have been transformative. Since the lawsuit was filed as a class action of all authors and publishers against Google, the settlement would also incorporate all parties, even those that were not directly involved in the suit. Google, on the other hand, would have to pay a substantial amount to settle the case, but it would have the right to build a digital library of all the books it had digitized.

Richard Sarnoff pointed out the benefits to the publishers in the proposed Google settlement by saying, "I had always thought it made no sense to literally sue this into oblivion. We wanted to find out how as an industry to make this work, to find out how to light up for the twenty-first century all of these fiction and nonfiction books."[22] Sarnoff frankly admitted that the publishers had a great deal to gain from mass digitization. They had been concerned for a long time about the great number of books that were out of print but still in copyright. Publishers did not have a good mechanism for making those works discoverable to readers other than digitizing the books and making them available on their organizational websites. Digitization was costly. Publishers were not set up to do that work. Most importantly, they did not know if the demand for these older works would justify the expense of digitizing them. They worried, though, about finding an economic model that would compensate the authors and the publishers for their intellectual property.

No one can say exactly why Judge Chin did not accept the agreement that the three parties proposed. Looking back, it continues to be a sad chapter. James Somers, as he assessed events from his 2017 perspective, noted that publishers faced a

22. Sarnoff, interview.

dilemma. Even if they won statutory damages, those were likely to be minimal. But scanned snippets might drive user demand for out-of-print books. They found themselves in a situation in which they did not want to lose the lawsuit, but they didn't want to win it either.[23] The benefits of a settlement would not have been enormous for publishers, but they would have been truly significant for the ordinary information seeker.

Headwinds

In the beginning, it looked as if the proposed settlement would be a success. All parties had reached an agreement they were happy with. The presiding judge, Denny Chin, issued a call for responses to the proposed settlement, and many respondents came forward.

For competitors of Google—most notably Microsoft but at the time also Amazon and Yahoo—it was troubling that Google would control a database of all the books ever published. Already the dominant search engine, Google could also become the only legal mechanism for mining digital out-of-print books. Microsoft worried that the connection to digital books would further strengthen Google's competitive place in the search engine race. While competitors could also make deals with libraries to digitize their collections, Amazon was not as concerned about the monopoly on digitized content as it was about the prospect of Google building an enormous digital bookstore. With the ability to sell those books, Google would be able to establish a massive bookstore and would have the advantage of not having to clear rights to out-of-print books on

---

23. Somers, "Torching the Modern-Day Library of Alexandria."

a title-by-title basis. In addition, libraries would not have any incentive to go through the process a second time.

Although librarians had been excited about the prospect of increasing access to out-of-print books, some scholars and librarians, most notably Robert Darnton, began to worry that the settlement was akin to making a bargain with the devil. The Google book digitization project would create the world's largest library but at the expense, perhaps, of creating the largest bookstore, too, one managed by a powerful monopolist.[24]

The doubts aired by Darnton regarding the knowledge found in books being held by a corporate entity resonated with many scholars, as well as librarians. The library community was already in a contentious relationship with commercial publishers because of the high prices they were being charged for journal subscriptions. The Google partners, inexplicably to a number of librarians, had given Google unrestricted access to their book collections. Would not the Google deal simply mean that librarians would have to buy back the books they had loaned to Google for scanning? The library partners were, perhaps unexpectedly to many, going to provide the raw materials to allow Google to sell access to books. But the key question was what it would mean in terms of price and monopoly. Although scholars, and by extension research libraries, would have benefited from the proposed settlement, not all librarians were as enthusiastic as the original Google partner libraries. A number of scholars expressed concerns about a corporate entity's ability to influence search results through its search algorithm, giving that corporation too much control over access to knowledge.

24. Ibid.

Others feared that a corporation could privilege economic incentive over users' privacy.[25]

Although the major library organizations—the American Library Association, the Association of College and Research Libraries, and the Association of Research Libraries—did not oppose the proposed settlement, they sent a strongly worded letter warning Judge Chin of the dangers of the settlement. They cited concerns about a corporation being able to censor content, its ability to price gouge, and its ability to invade the privacy of readers.[26] The joint letter sent to Judge Chin focuses on the values espoused by the library organizations rather than the benefits to readers and researchers. The library organizations raised enough questions about monopolistic behaviors of Google that the Justice Department began an investigation into the matter.

One of the Google partners took a pragmatic approach. Paul Courant recalls that "Bob [Darnton] . . . worried that Google would set prices to maximize profits. Once again, they are going to nick a big vein and we will bleed money. My view from an economist's perspective was that the equilibrium price in the Google bookstore would be very low. There is not a big demand for scholarly monographs, and we were going to get to the Holy Grail. The books would not be free; the price would be pretty good. The big difference between Bob and me is that Bob was afraid to cede control to a corporation. I never trusted Google. I would like to have a higher opinion of human nature. I thought the economics were such that the product would be

25. Siva Vaidhyanathan, "A Risky Gamble with Google," *Chronicle of Higher Education*, December 2, 2005, B7–10.

26. Ryan Singel, "Libraries Warn of Censorship, Privacy, Cost in Google's Digital Library," *Wired*, May 5, 2009, https://www.wired.com/2009/05/libraries-warn-of-censorship-privacy-cost-in-googles-digital-library/.

enormously valuable to the public. I trusted the marketplace. Economists don't trust companies. We trust the public to discipline them."[27]

Courant saw the settlement as the lesser evil. He needed to digitize the University of Michigan collections to meet the emerging needs of researchers and scholars. He could not afford to establish a digitization lab and do the work in-house. In a lengthy piece, titled "On Being in Bed with Google,"[28] he explained why the proposed settlement seemed the most palatable course of action.

Publishers clearly favored the settlement. Richard Sarnoff wistfully recalled, "I wish it had turned out differently with the first settlement—it would have been the crowning achievement of my career, of my life."[29] For the publishing community, the settlement would have created a digital library system that kept the publishers as central players who maintained control of their intellectual property.

The Settlement Fails

Pamela Samuelson, University of California Law School professor, observed that the "'proposed settlement looked like a win-win-win: the libraries would get access to millions of books, Google would be able to recoup its investment in the Google book digitization project, and authors and publishers would get a new revenue stream from books that had been yielding zero returns. And legislation would be unnecessary to bring about

27. Courant, interview.
28. http://paulcourant.net/2007/11/04/on-being-in-bed-with-google/.
29. Sarnoff, interview.

this result.'"[30] But in the end the Court rejected this settlement agreement.

Ultimately, the U.S. Department of Justice voiced its concerns with the settlement agreement from an antitrust perspective. Even though the settlement was characterized as non-exclusive, the Department of Justice pointed out that it would be highly unlikely that another company would attempt to scan so many books in order to build its own database and search service. The lawyers wrote, "It is an attempt to use the class-action mechanism to implement forward-looking business arrangements that go far beyond the dispute before the Court in this litigation."[31] With the Justice Department recommending against the settlement, the Court rejected it and sent it back to the parties to renegotiate.

Instead of the settlement agreement that would have yielded a robust marketplace, for better and for worse around digital monographs, the parties came together with a revised settlement agreement that was far more narrowly scoped. Not only did Google fail to win a fair use victory, it did not manage to generate a marketplace that could have significantly expanded access to and the impact of the book in the digital era, unlocking value that was bound inside the printed codex. Instead, Google agreed to a settlement that limited dramatically its rights to use the in-copyright materials. While it was able to continue providing search for them, it was unable to offer a complete access solution. In a strange parallel, the existing publishers and select third parties were to steadily expand their digital offerings, the frontlist materials available digitally both through Amazon for consumers and through site licenses

---

30. Somers, "Torching the Modern-Day Library of Alexandria."
31. https://www.justice.gov/atr/case-document/file/488171/download.

for academic and corporate customers. Still, today, librarians' efforts to rethink the role of the monograph and reconsider collections management are to a great degree stifled by the backlist works that remain digitally unavailable due to copyright considerations.

AN UNREALIZED DREAM

Digital technology created great excitement about the possible public good uses. As digital technology's capabilities were becoming evident, several public figures pointed to the prospects for a universal digital library, without taking into account any of the obstacles posed by copyright law. President Bill Clinton in his 1998 State of the Union Address said, "It is time to build . . . an America where every child can stretch a hand across a keyboard and reach every book ever written, every painting ever painted, every symphony ever composed."[32] University of Michigan president Mary Sue Coleman, in her address to the Association of American Publishers in 2006, expressed similar hopes by saying, "Our venture will result in a magnitude of discovery that seems almost incomprehensible."

Had the settlement been approved, one can imagine that Google could have become a national, comprehensive digital library, with public libraries being access points in the library cosmos. Regrettably, the bold idea the founders of Google had for making all the world's knowledge accessible was not to be realized. The disregard for copyright status of the books ultimately led to the legal quarrels with publishers and authors, and even though the proceedings would ultimately stall and

32. https://millercenter.org/the-presidency/presidential-speeches/january-27
-1998-state-union-address.

Google would eventually move on to other non-book "moon-shot" projects, the light that was shined on out-of-print but still in-copyright books—"orphan works"—would have long-term effects in the library and scholarly worlds.

LOOKING BACK ON THE SETTLEMENT

Google invested millions with no prospect of revenue, and it was only after the legal challenges were mounted and a settlement proposed that Google could imagine a revenue stream. It is fanciful now to think about what might have happened had the Google settlement been approved by the courts, although law professor James Grimmelmann wrote extensively about how the proposed settlement could have benefited Google, libraries, and the broader academic community. In essence, Grimmelmann proposed that the settlement be reshaped so that the Book Search project would be publicly controlled.[33] Some of the visionaries who had been willing to risk a partnership with Google could imagine a transformation in the information ecosystem, going beyond mass digitization and the proposed settlement to the whole system of scholarly communication. Paul Courant in wistful hindsight regretted that he had not become a provost sooner. Perhaps the system of scholarly communication would now be different. He said, "I regret that I got to the library a year too late. We [the academic community] should have bought Blackwell rather than let Wiley do it. I didn't know enough then to know that if HathiTrust had been in business then, we could have done it."[34] Courant

33. James Grimmelmann, "How to Fix the Google Book Search Settlement," *Journal of Internet Law* 12, no. 10 (April 2009).
34. Courant, interview.

imagined a world in which information producers, not the large commercial publishers, could control the distribution system for at least the humanistic portions of scholarly research.

John Wilkin now imagines that had the settlement been approved, libraries, collectively, would have made far more progress on developing a universal digital library: "We would have seen a very different cost and benefit in all of this. Google would still be digitizing in-copyright materials and at a greater volume because they would have seen an ability to profit from those materials going forward. We would have done more. We might have approached the questions of comprehensiveness more passionately. And institutions such as Michigan would be benefiting much more significantly from the corpus because it would have had access to the majority of in-copyright materials through a license at no or low cost."[35] Wilkin expanded this view by speculating that if the library community had had assurances that it could license materials easily, it would have been considerably easier to imagine solutions to the shared-print for books problem.

Mark Sandler, another librarian at the University of Michigan at the launch of the Google book digitization project, continues to regret that the settlement was not approved: "It could have been a way better world to have in-copyright and out-of-copyright materials, publisher-contributed material and library-digitized material, in one centrally managed space, operated at scale by people who actually know something about discovery and could improve it continuously based on user behavior. I was very enthusiastic about the settlement and thought it had tremendous value. I thought libraries would

35. Wilkin, interview.

be willing to pay for that value. I did not believe that Google was actually doing the project for the money."[36]

All of those at the University of Michigan viewed the settlement as a way to give libraries a shared purpose: to make information more widely available to all. Others, notably the library associations, saw real danger in the proposed settlement. When the courts rejected the proposal, all parties had to rethink their plans for a digital library.

Other Concerns

Librarians were not alone in expressing concerns about a corporation having such an influential role in scholarly communication. The Electronic Frontier Foundation (EFF) is notable for its concern about privacy in a world in which technology played an increasingly important role. The EFF was formed in the early 1990s by a small group of technologists who grew alarmed about the possibility of government's use of technology to gain access to information that traditionally would have been protected by laws of free speech and privacy. The United States Secret Service conducted a series of raids in trying to track down the source of a document illegally obtained from a BellSouth computer that described the operational details of the 911 emergency system. The government feared that once this information was available, hackers could take over the system and use the lines that were supposed to be dedicated to true emergencies. The Secret Service raided Steve Jackson Games (SJGames), a small games book publisher in Austin, Texas, in an attempt to find copies of the illegal document and removed all of the computers from the business. Without access

36. Sandler, interview.

to his computers, Steve Jackson faced financial ruin, causing him to lay off nearly half of his staff. When the Secret Service returned the computers eventually, the staff noticed something very strange: all of the electronic mail, including non-employee users' personal messages to one another, had been accessed and deleted. Jackson was deeply concerned that his rights as a publisher had been violated and the free speech and privacy rights of his users had been abridged. He made inquiries to civil liberties groups to seek legal representation but discovered that in those early days of technological development, such groups were not yet prepared to argue his case.[37]

The concern for privacy in the electronic era emerged again during the Google Book settlement discussions. In August 2009, the Electronic Frontier Foundation, on its website, issued a call to publishers to join the foundation in objecting to the proposed settlement. EFF argued that Google's tracking on online book browsing would have a "chilling effect" on authors' readership. EFF argued that "the settlement does not sufficiently protect authors and publishers because it fails to provide the same privacy protections for readers in the digital world that apply to reading physical books from libraries, bookstores, etc. These include protections from subpoenas, law enforcement investigations, and other forms of surveillance and profiling."[38] The foundation harkened back to the role of public libraries in protecting patrons' right to privacy, noting that librarians have a professional ethical responsibility to protect the privacy of readers.

---

37. https://www.eff.org/about/history.

38. https://www.eff.org/issues/privacy/google-book-search-settlement-for-authors-and-publishers.

Although the privacy issues raised by EFF did not galvanize the scholarly community at the time the Google settlement was under discussion, they subsequently became more central to the library community.

Google Reassesses

Although the proposed settlement offered some benefits to all parties, perhaps it could have been forecast that it would never work. For the library community, a self-appointed for-profit company, even one with a more noble mission statement, was hard to accept as the appropriate builder of a universal library. The best result, however, for the library community was that the goal of digitizing collections now seemed possible. Collaborative ventures that had formed in Google's wake were emboldened to take on greater ambition, and more libraries joined in. The Digital Public Library of America, proposed by Robert Darnton, enticed public libraries, historical societies, and museums to join library partners to develop a database of digital holdings that would, at least theoretically, constitute a broad-based digital library.

The libraries that had allowed Google to digitize their collections now held copies of their digital collections, and it made sense to most of them to join with other institutions in similar circumstances to develop a centralized collection of digital materials. HathiTrust, based at the University of Michigan, has grown from a handful of institutions to 125 member organizations working together to amass digital books that are accessible to all of their faculty and students.

Even the Library of Congress changed course when Carla Hayden was sworn in to lead it in July 2016. The focus for the library became public access to its collections, and digitization was the vehicle for that access.

Despite the many efforts under way to achieve something akin to Google's vision, the results continue to pale in comparison to Google's. Financial resources account for some of the slow progress, but equally to blame are the many conversations and governance issues that inevitably accompany collaborative projects.

Some of the visionaries who had such high hopes for the universal digital library hold out hope that a fire can be lit to reignite the effort, this time as a library-led project. Paul Courant of Michigan is not ready to give up, even though he says "mass digitization is dead." He adds, "We are back in that place where we do deals with various entities that want to digitize things, where we allow them to give us copies in a few years. We get the miscellaneous grant from Mellon to digitize. We have done well with hidden collections. But all the holes didn't get filled. We still don't have good solutions for preservation of current stuff. Now we are in Zeno's paradox. Nobody wants to pay for it."[39]

Copyright law continues to plague efforts toward a national digital library. Mass digitization is dead because after the Google episode, few nonprofit organizations are willing to take the risk of digitizing material that was published after 1923. The Library of Congress made an attempt in the spring of 2005 to look carefully at the need to revise Section 108 of the copyright law and assembled a diverse group of stakeholders to make recommendations. The Section 108 Study Group was convened under the aegis of the National Digital Information

39. Courant, interview.

Infrastructure and Preservation Program (NDIIPP) and the U.S. Copyright Office. The group was asked to make recommendations to the Librarian of Congress and the Register of Copyrights by mid-2007 on possible revisions of the law that reflect reasonable uses of copyrighted works by libraries and archives in the digital age. The group was asked to strike an appropriate balance between copyright holders and libraries and archives in a manner that best serves the public interest. The convenors of the group observed that the increasing use of digital media prompted the study, as digital technology had radically transformed how copyrighted works are created and disseminated and also how libraries and archives preserve these works.

Section 108 of the copyright law that provided limited exceptions for libraries and archives to make copies in specified instances for preservation, replacement, and patron access was drafted in the era of analog materials. In the digital world even the word "copy" carries a different meaning. The Section 108 Study Group was commissioned to review and document how Section 108 should be revised in light of the changes wrought by digital technologies. The study group, composed of copyright experts from various fields, including law, publishing, libraries, archives, film, music, software, and photography, was co-chaired by Laura Gasaway, associate dean for academic affairs and professor of law at the University of North Carolina, and Richard Rudick, former vice president and general counsel of John Wiley & Sons.

The study group met for two days a month for nearly a year longer than expected. Their final report was released on March 31, 2008. Not surprisingly, with such a diverse group, there was not complete agreement on what should be done. Many of the sections report that the topic was discussed, but no agreement was reached on a recommendation. Without a clear signal of unanimity from the stakeholders, Congress has not taken action on revising Section 108. Libraries and archives remain uncertain about what can and cannot be digitized and made widely accessible to the public.

Publishers' business models depend upon controlling their intellectual property. They, understandably, do not see a future for themselves if all content is freely available. Their contributions to scholarship include peer review, extensive editing, distribution, and marketing. These functions cannot be accomplished at no cost.

In the final analysis, a robust, national digital library of the kind with which Google enticed us will be possible only when publishers and libraries and archives recognize that they are part of the same ecosystem and the survival of each of them is inextricably tied to the others.

7

Seeking Complementarities

THE EMERGENCE OF HATHITRUST

With the failure of the ambitious settlement agreement, the prospect of radically democratizing access to these digitized materials ended. Efforts to build strong alternatives to Google's initiative were having only limited traction, as we saw in chapter 5. So, Google's program was the strongest there was among the efforts to build the Universal Library but much weaker than it might have been. With this looming reality, efforts to build strong complements to Google's efforts that would maximize its strategic potential took on greater importance.

At the same time, there was ample reason to wonder if the library community was prepared to provide such a complement. As we saw in chapter 3, libraries lacked the structure for strong collective engagement with a partner like Google, which preferred to work on a one-on-one basis under nondisclosure agreements. In the end, a favored few libraries had the opportunity to partner with Google and, in the process, dramatically accelerate their own digital efforts. For most libraries individually, the Google book digitization project was simply a phenomenon to be watched. Notwithstanding these structural impediments, several key visionaries saw to it that HathiTrust was created.[1]

The Andrew W. Mellon Foundation

The Mellon Foundation was the organization most likely to be the catalyst for both the library and publishing communities. It had been one of the leaders in fostering the development of digital libraries and platforms, building on its legacy of support for libraries and humanistic scholarship. When the foundation invested millions in the development of JSTOR and ArtStor, it was not simply undertaking a library project. It was facilitating a collaborative endeavor that involved libraries, publishers, and scholars in identifying the most important journal literature to support humanistic scholarship and teaching for all institutions of higher education, to digitize that material at the foundation's expense for easy access by the scholarly community, while still protecting the business model of publishers for their current material.

Mellon had spent several intervening years developing its program to advance digital tools across libraries and the humanities. In 1999, it hired Donald J. Waters, then the director of the Digital Library Federation, to lead its work in libraries and scholarly communications. Mellon did not pursue a comprehensive, unified digital library on a grand scale. Rather, in keeping with the foundation's general policy of acting on the

---

1. For another version of this history, see Alissa Centivany, "The Dark History of HathiTrust," *Proceedings of the 50th Hawaii International Conference on System Sciences,* 2017, https://ir.lib.uwo.ca/fimspub/120/.

proposals received from the academic community, Waters took a more decentralized approach. Under his leadership, Mellon invested approximately $750 million in 1,800 grants over a period of 20 years, funding the development of tools and infrastructure, as well as the creation of numerous digital works for specific scholarly communities.

When confronted by Google's mass digitization project, the foundation made attempts to collaborate with the corporation, or at least offer advice for how the major research libraries could develop an alternative partnership. The foundation's enormous resources, and its leadership through JSTOR in bringing together libraries and publishers, suggested that it should have a central role in any mass digitization initiative. But the Google project advanced without Mellon, as would HathiTrust.

The Library of Congress

From its creation, the Library of Congress has struggled with identity. It was established to support the needs of legislators, but after the library was destroyed by the British in the War of 1812, Congress agreed to purchase the private library of Thomas Jefferson, which was the largest and most comprehensive collection in the United States. Jefferson collected in three broad categories: memory, imagination, and reason. One of Jefferson's quotes that has propelled the library's desire to be a national library is "there is in fact no subject to which a member of Congress may not have occasion to refer."[2]

Even though the Library of Congress has never been officially designated a national library, it has provided national

2. https://www.loc.gov/exhibits/jefferson/jefflib.html.

leadership for the library community for decades, especially in providing bibliographic information. When the library launched its National Digital Information Infrastructure and Preservation Program, it expected that the library community would support its development of the National Digital Library. Early congressional appropriations and private philanthropic gifts provided reasons to believe that many more people would have instantaneous access to the world's knowledge. At least some librarians thought that national leadership from the Library of Congress would keep the development of a universal digital library in the hands of knowledgeable librarians. Ultimately, the convoluted legislative appropriations process did not deliver the funds that might have made the Library of Congress a reasonable substitute, but it was no match for Google's agility and deep pockets. Even though the Library of Congress joined collaborative projects such as the Digital Library Federation, it did not assume a leadership role. Rather, it focused on its internal priorities of developing American Memory, a digital library of primary source materials related to American history, and the World Digital Library, an international initiative to collect cultural heritage materials most representative of different countries and regions. The changing priorities of Congress resulted in funds originally promised not to be delivered, and the glimmering possibility that the Library of Congress would work harmoniously with other libraries to develop a distributed national digital library slowly faded.

The Research Library Community

The research library community does not have a natural organization for forming alliances and working together. The Association of Research Libraries, a membership organization of the

124 largest libraries in North America, necessarily focuses on the topics that are of great concern to most of the members. In the late 1990s, digital libraries were not the highest priority for many of the member organizations. The Library of Congress's rhetoric about becoming the National Digital Library left a number of the research institutions that had begun to explore digital library creation feeling that their collections were not being recognized as part of the national collection. The largest research libraries formed the Digital Library Federation, which could have been a model for distributed collections serving as a national collection, but the group focused more on the technical obstacles to digital library development and did not attempt to serve as a coordinating agent for all libraries, so the voluntary efforts had no real authority.

Several major initiatives developed around both discovery and access. These initiatives sought complementarity by focusing not on publications but rather on ensuring that the special collections libraries were digitizing could be more readily discovered, including Australia's Trove, the EU's Europeana, and the Digital Public Library of America.

Ultimately, HathiTrust grew out of the vacuum in community leadership that became evident following the tectonic shake-up caused by Google. HathiTrust sought to build a suite of transformative services for research libraries and their academic users. Relying on the precepts of copyright law rather than a negotiated settlement, the transformation would have different contours and more notable limits. HathiTrust has accomplished a great deal, but it has treaded carefully, not attempting to serve as the unifying voice of library coordination around collections and collaborative transformation. Instead, a panoply of membership organizations has grown up in parallel, each claiming some right to bandwidth and agenda setting, including several that survived for only a few years. Nevertheless, the development of HathiTrust, the library-controlled platform for the preservation and provision of access to digitized collections, is a signal moment in the story of large-scale digitization. The story of its creation demonstrates amply just how difficult it is to achieve shared clarity of purpose in cross-institutional academic collaboration.

HathiTrust

As we saw in chapter 3, before a single book was digitized or the Google digitization program announced, Michigan's John Wilkin was already looking for funding to support a library-controlled platform for the digitized materials. Success stories are so often presented as inevitable or obvious, but the development of HathiTrust involved several key contingencies. One plumb line ran through from its earliest conceptualization: that there should be "a shared, distributed resource" for the libraries to store the digitized versions of their collections.[3] Beyond this, key choices were made about its basic service model, how it would be organized, who would provide its funding, and how it would be governed, and, had timing or circumstances differed, several of these choices could well have been resolved differently.

HathiTrust was unique. It was the unusual library collaboration that was not started up with initial capital from a third-party funder, such as the Institute of Museum and Library Services or the Andrew W. Mellon Foundation. This added to the aggravation of its founding in no small measure. Where other start-up collaborative squabbles are often resolved by a

---

3. This was clear as early as May 2004. Wilkin, memorandum.

program officer or a grant peer review process, in this case the question of who would be a founder was very much on the table for an uncomfortable period of time. Motives were questioned, tempers flared, and bad feelings lingered. For all the stereotypes of librarian complaisance, HathiTrust's founding was no less dramatic than that of many other start-ups, and perhaps more so because of the underlying layer of academic politics. But, notwithstanding all this drama, with the universities having to put skin in the game from the onset, HathiTrust emerged with a strong sense of strategic direction and community ownership, a rare and valuable combination.

"The Nose under the Tent": Library Rights

A fundamental aspect of the initial digitization agreements between Google and its library partners was that a copy of the digitization output files, including the page images and OCR, would be delivered to the libraries.[4] Michigan was at the forefront of seeking this clause and then suggesting to the other libraries that they do so as well.

Versions of such agreements are fairly standard in library digitization partnerships with commercial firms, such as those that ProQuest, Gale, and Readex have negotiated with a variety of libraries in building special collections. In these arrangements, with the underlying material typically out of copyright, the library agreements would regularly include an embargo of ten years or more during which the commercial partner would

---

4. Some institutions, such as Michigan and Wisconsin, insisted on receiving both public domain and in-copyright materials. Some other institutions would initially ask Google to hold in-copyright materials for them "in escrow," presumably to avoid the risk and liability of holding in-copyright files.

have the exclusive right to provide online access. After the embargo, the library would have the right to make the materials publicly available online.

In the Google partnership agreements, the libraries negotiated for stronger provisions associated with access, in particular, than had been common with these other vendor partnerships. The Google partner libraries not only would have a copy of the digitization output files returned to them for future use but also would be able to make the materials available for online access immediately. There were certain restrictions. Some limitations would be necessary for in-copyright materials. In addition, the library partners were prohibited from sharing the materials for indexing and discovery purposes with Google competitors, but they could use the files in collaborative agreements with other libraries.

Another key provision was that these agreements explicitly permitted the libraries to use the digitization outputs collaboratively. For example, the University of Michigan's agreement with Google specifically indicated that the Michigan copy could be used by the university itself as well as in "Cooperative Web Services . . . as part of services offered in cooperation with partner research libraries such as the institutions of the Digital Library Federation."[5] Courant describes this "tiny clause" and its mention of "consortial activities" as "the nose under the tent" that made it possible for libraries "to use our collections to share with others."[6] Wilkin recalls that, notwithstanding the nondisclosure agreements then in place, Michigan

---

5. This language can be found in section 4.4.2 of the cooperative agreement, available at http://www.lib.umich.edu/sites/default/files/services/mdp/um-google -cooperative-agreement.pdf.

6. Courant, interview.

coordinated with other potential Google partner institutions from the very beginning to develop coordinated contractual language enabling collaboration.[7]

Objectives

The initial motivating objective of Michigan and its partners that would found HathiTrust was preservation of the digitized output files. To be sure, Google had a massive infrastructure and growing operation, and there was little immediate technical or business risk. But some of the partners feared that Google's interests might shift over time, and it was a young company in a rapidly changing market. As CDL's Laine Farley recalled, Google was "very clear that preservation was not their goal," and so "we didn't want it to be that we were entirely dependent on Google for access to the digitized copies."[8] If the libraries were to achieve the strategic opportunities that they foresaw from the partnership, greater assurances would be needed with respect to long-term preservation and access. They needed an absolute backstop where the digitized files could be retained and preserved.

In this respect, the libraries' thinking was very similar to that of the Andrew W. Mellon Foundation when its leaders began to plan the service that would become JSTOR. In the early stages of that initiative, the objective was to strategically transform libraries' approaches to collections management, "miniaturizing" the space requirements for storing ever-growing journal backfiles. To rely on a digitized version provided online, rather than the tangible printed copies stored locally, it was clear that

7. Wilkin, interview.
8. Farley, interview.

provisions for long-term access, including preservation, would have to be provided.[9]

It was too soon to know the exact nature of the library transformations that a broader mass digitization initiative would unlock, but there was no question that many of the libraries most excited about the Google book digitization project saw the need for high-quality preservation. And, while Internet Archive was seen at least by some as doing so for its library digitization partnerships, no such not-for-profit organization was in place for the Google book digitization outputs. It would be essential that libraries find another way to ensure the preservation of the digital files created through the Google book digitization project.

Michigan Commits

From the beginning, Michigan was determined to retain a local copy of the digital files. As we saw in chapter 2, Wilkin first went to the Andrew W. Mellon Foundation to seek funding to support a repository, either for itself or through the nascent ITHAKA organization,[10] but when Mellon leadership learned about the Google digitization partnership their interest turned toward the digitization itself and the opportunities and problems associated with Google's involvement, rather than the preservation considerations, and no repository funding was ever provided. Instead, Michigan proceeded at first on its own.

---

9. See Schonfeld, *JSTOR: A History*, chap. 2, esp. p. 37.

10. "We would also request funds to support the development of a cooperative governance organization, though would be glad to see that effort led by Ithaka." Wilkin, memorandum.

There was some question initially about whether Michigan could take this work on itself or would need to "outsource" it to an organization with greater technical skills than a library. Even if there would be a variety of investigations about how and with what partners to take on this work, it was Wilkin who felt that the library could lead rather than outsource. Thinking about not only Michigan but also a select group of peer research universities, Wilkin would recall that "we all believed we could do these things—we were doing these things—at some scale."[11]

At the same time, Wilkin was not naive about what the effort would require. He had already undertaken detailed budget planning and option development for such a storage and preservation solution by May 2004.[12] As Courant recalls, "John had the profound insight that it would be expensive."[13] Recognizing up front the likely nature of the costs made possible some important choices that would seed the development of HathiTrust.

Having institutional support from the provost was critical. First, the library saved up some "end of year money" from its library's budget for initial hardware expenses. The idea was to create a "dark archive" just to park Michigan's copy for the time being. But it was clear that one-time funding was insufficient for the nature of the need. Wilkin's analysis made it possible for Courant as provost to allocate recurring funding for storage and preservation. "I committed a recurring line that was sufficient to store the Michigan digitization project. It was important that I was then the provost. I committed three-quarters of a million a year to do this. . . . Having that budget line enabled us to make

11. Wilkin, interview.
12. Wilkin, memorandum.
13. Courant, interview.

this commitment. And this allowed us to keep our own copy of the collection." Others might not have seen the importance of such a recurring investment.[14]

Thus Michigan invested in its own local repository of the digitized content. The people at Michigan—a provost who was invested in digital libraries and a technologist with a strong interest in developing digital capacities—made progress possible.

Beyond a Single Institution

Even if libraries such as Michigan could each manage the preservation of their own digitized files, many other academic libraries preferred a collaborative approach. In Wilkin's initial outreach to Mellon, he had a clear vision of some kind of cross-institutional partnership or collaboration. He explained the problems with a single institution working on its own:

> Doing so would miss critical opportunities that relate to collaboration, shared collections, and the relationship between our print and digital collections. Of course, very few of the items held by Michigan are held uniquely. If a number of institutions partner in a way that we collectively own these digital copies, we can benefit together from a whole host of downstream changes in the way we do our work. Through the creation of a shared repository, including shared rights management (e.g., which institutions have access to which in-copyright volumes?), the volumes would serve as surrogates for printed materials, providing radically improved access to our collections and opportunities for shared

14. Ibid.

services, and can help us re-focus our efforts with regard to the storage of print materials.[15]

Even before the Google project was announced, Wilkin had a clear vision that a collaborative approach would offer the greatest transformational potential. But there was an even more practical reason than this. Having recognized that the expenditure for storage and preservation would be recurring also shifted Michigan's thinking. Rather than seeing the effort as requiring a one-off capital expenditure for hardware, Michigan leadership knew that there would be recurring costs to preserve and provide access to the content. They had a vested interest in controlling the costs that would recur. "This helped us think about long-range cost efficiency."[16] And that in turn led Michigan leaders to focus on the economic as well as other benefits of cross-institutional collaboration.

Perhaps Michigan could have developed and managed the repository on its own. But there were both strategic and budgetary rationales to build a collaboration.

Turning to the Big Ten

For some time, John Wilkin had been adapting the initial proposal for a shared digital repository. At one point, it was pitched as a Michigan-California partnership, and Wilkin recalls this was the first proposal for a specific collaboration that he developed. Perhaps because of challenges in corralling the various UC institutions together, this proposal does not appear to have

15. Wilkin, memorandum.
16. Courant, interview.

gone anywhere.[17] Next he turned to a peer group largely aligned with the Big Ten, a group that has a long and largely successful history of collaborations.

As the academic, library, and purchasing collaboration vehicle for the Big Ten institutions (plus the University of Chicago), the Committee on Institutional Cooperation (the CIC; subsequently renamed the Big Ten Academic Alliance) brought to bear a group of largely flagship state universities with major research enterprises and important academic libraries. In addition to Michigan, a second CIC member, Wisconsin, had joined the Google digitization partnership, so there was reason to suspect that a shared repository could make sense.[18] Discussions with CIC library directors and library alliance executive director Mark Sandler suggested there could be real interest in "a major collaboration" that would see CIC serve as the collaboration vehicle for the shared digital repository.[19]

As the group explored the possibility, it looked into a variety of options for how such a repository collaboration could be developed. While there was some overall support for the collaboration, there was also some of what Sandler would recall as "the usual hedging that you get in a collaborative effort."[20] There were two broad areas of disagreement.

First, there was a desire to reduce costs and reduce the burden on CIC library budgets. Some were interested in reducing

17. "The original idea was that Michigan and California—folks at CDL will tell you that it never left Dan's desk so no one knew that they were talking since 2004. The second iteration was through the CIC." Wilkin, interview.

18. "At first Michigan and Wisconsin were looking for a way to build a shared infrastructure/service for the CIC. There was little motivation then to see it as a common interest." Sandler, interview.

19. Ibid.

20. Roger C. Schonfeld, interview with Mark Sandler, July 27, 2017.

costs, perhaps by having only one instance of the storage architecture rather than the proposed two, or working with an existing entity rather than a new collaboration. One director was opposed out of a sense that storage and access through Google would suffice. Others felt that since the vast majority of the Google-digitized content from CIC libraries was really Michigan's, it was unreasonable for their libraries to be asked to support this repository in any substantial way. The basic question was, "Why would I put money in to solve Michigan's problem?"

This concern would diminish as additional universities began to join the Google digitization partnership. Notably, Mark Sandler was able to secure a master arrangement for all the member institutions of what was then known as the Committee on Institutional Cooperation (CIC) to join the digitization partnership. Perhaps this would help with the eventual decision of CIC to partner on HathiTrust.

The second, and in some ways more basic, question was whether this "shared" effort was a collaboration of equals. Michigan had spent years planning the technical architecture and was going to be building the infrastructure, which irritated some by taking an approach that was seen as insufficiently consultative for a supposed collaboration. At least one director wondered if Michigan would end up controlling the files of all libraries. There was a fairly broad concern that Michigan was not signaling an interest in launching a real collaboration; at least one director voiced the sense that Michigan might be acting more like a vendor.

There was conceptual support from most CIC library directors, but exactly how to turn this Michigan-spearheaded initiative into a true collaboration was unclear at best. In early November 2007, there was a meeting of the CIC library directors in Urbana-Champaign, Illinois, and prominent on the agenda was the CIC shared digital repository. In a morning session, two fundamental concerns were raised. Reflecting on the conversations that led up to this change in direction, John Wilkin remembers that the shared digital repository was "near failure."[21]

The process of engaging CIC had failed. But rather than abandon the vision, Wilkin and his allies simply abandoned the process and took matters into their own hands.

On returning from lunch, there was an announcement. Indiana and Michigan were prepared to fund the repository themselves. It would be made available for other institutions to use, including CIC members, which could join this effort or elect not to do so. Courant notes that many of his fellow "CIC librarians were really pissed at the time. I said we were going ahead to develop a coalition of the willing."[22] Mark Sandler describes it as an "ugly, ugly meeting."[23]

Forcing Change

With Courant and Wilkin having long grown frustrated with the progress being made in establishing a CIC shared digital repository, Wilkin had by summer 2007 (before this difficult CIC directors meeting) begun working on a business plan for a different kind of model. This document not only was key in turning Michigan away from the CIC collaboration model but also contains significant and fairly raw reflections from a key Hathi founder.

21. Wilkin, interview.
22. Courant, interview.
23. Sandler, interview, December 22, 2016.

Although the attempt to gain acceptance from all CIC members of the importance of a universal digital library had been unsuccessful, Wilkin turned his attention to the Google partner libraries on the one hand and academic libraries broadly on the other. In the absence of some kind of shared community repository, Wilkin feared that mass digitization would not be a transformative innovation for academic libraries but rather strategically stillborn: "The project managers at each of the participating Google partner institutions confirmed their intent to build separate and disconnected repositories. Without a transformational model, libraries will be doomed to replicate the mistakes of print libraries in the digital space." He was ultimately concerned that an ongoing local focus on collections rather than systemwide preservation and access would impede the transition to finding means for adding greater value. He was clear that without a paradigm driven by shared infrastructure, libraries will select for "local autonomy" even when it yields "bad solutions" to "reliability," redundancy," and ultimately preservation.[24]

In his thinking, Wilkin was concerned about the strategic repositioning of libraries, and he had come to accept that the kind of collaborative model being explored with the CIC "will fail . . . achieving mediocrity and muddled direction." He was convinced that "creating a new model for libraries will not happen through influence and organizing collective action, but by forcing change." The CIC "cooperative model with a complex governance process" was the wrong vehicle for forcing change. Out of a sense of urgency and focus, he therefore envisioned "a model for an accessible archive, one owned and operated by the University of Michigan Library for the purpose of serving

24. Ibid.

the broader library community." In this UM-owned model, the impact of the repository would extend well beyond CIC.[25]

As Sandler would reflect, Michigan was able "to get things moving."[26]

Launching a Shared Digital Repository

While Michigan was clearly taking the lead, the Wilkin business model examined whether it could move forward alone. If it was seen to be essential to have two geographically dispersed instances of the storage architecture from a preservation perspective, costs were driven accordingly. And, running numbers about costs and impact, it became clear that some infusion of capital would be necessary beyond Michigan's current plans. An infusion of capital and a turn toward developing this repository as a service for the entire community would define the next steps.

By fall 2007, Courant and Wilkin had enlisted Indiana as their partner in the early development of HathiTrust. A second instance of the hardware infrastructure would be established at Indiana, which would contribute substantial resources to make this possible. In turn, Indiana would receive two of the five seats on the executive committee for this new undertaking.

A March 2008 contract between UM and CIC led to the launch of what soon became HathiTrust. CIC functioned as a second-stage investor, taking a role in governance.

By April, the shared digital repository contained 1.1 million volumes and 385 million pages of content, and there was

---

25. [John Wilkin], "Library Archive Repository Business Plan," August 1, 2007, HathiTrust files.

26. Sandler, interview, December 22, 2016.

mention of "high profile development efforts (e.g., collaboration with JSTOR)." Leaders were evaluating the possibility of loading vendor files (for example, from Gale) onto the platform. Finally, leaders considered naming options, including one that incorporated the biblical reference "Babel," but instead they chose to examine options related to memory, including elephants.[27]

In March it was unclear whether Hathi would provide for discovery beyond library catalogs, OCLC's worldcat.org, and Google. By June it was becoming increasingly clear that there would be at least one public interface to Hathi. And it seemed plausible that there could be just a single interface rather than separate ones for each member library's collections. This was a key strategic decision for the participating libraries being willing to think about a common collection.[28]

Once HathiTrust was up and running, it began to gather additional investor partners, but the politics around partnership were rarely simple. The University of California had previously been using a dark archive for preservation and had begun talking with other universities about some kind of mirroring options.[29] CDL's Laine Farley remembers "a fair number of concerns about whether we should join HathiTrust. To be kind of crass about it, a concern was that Michigan would get all the credit. We already had a digital preservation program, and we wanted to make sure that we had a stake in [HathiTrust] that was different [from other participants], that showed our contributions. John Wilkin to his credit said from the beginning

27. Agenda [including attachments], April 10, 2008, HathiTrust files.
28. "SDR Operational Advisory Board," June 11, 2008, HathiTrust files.
29. Farley, interview.

that it was important that other institutions could show their contributions to the infrastructure."[30] Enough of the individual university librarians of the UC campuses were ambivalent about joining that CDL had to cover most of its costs because otherwise they would not have participated.[31] By late 2008, though, UC was prepared in principle to join, subject to various commitments in terms of governance, preservation, technical and functional directions, content ingest, and public domain materials.[32] Although the official framing was that HathiTrust was formed as a partnership of CIC and UC, that was really very much a fiction.

At least in part, the partnership was related to the way in which libraries could jointly participate in the proposed settlement. Farley recalls that "the settlement agreement had been announced and Michigan was kind of pressuring us to be involved because we needed to show that we had a united front in weighing the terms of the settlement. We needed to show that we could take care of this if it all fell apart for some reason."[33] And in the coming months, a broader group of potential participants was being identified and tracked, including some from the East Coast, that would ultimately expand the partnership substantially.[34] Of course, the partnership was also related to concerns about preserving digital content.

30. Ibid.

31. Ibid.

32. University of California Libraries, "Letter of Intent to Join the HathiTrust," to HathiTrust Executive Committee, October 8, 2008, HathiTrust files.

33. Farley, interview.

34. Executive Committee governance discussion, October 24, 2008, HathiTrust files.

Organizing a Partnership

Recognizing that preservation was at the heart of the new service, the initiative brought together the Hindi word for elephant (with their long memories) and christened HathiTrust. It was the latest in a long line of library collaborative initiatives such as OCLC and JSTOR that were named without any reference to consumer branding principles.

Michigan made by far the biggest investment to capitalize Hathi and allow its operations to commence. With resources from within the library and an investment by the provost, Michigan was able to contribute more than half a million dollars annually in the initial years, with another substantial investment by Indiana University as well as smaller fees paid by other members after they joined. This infusion of working capital allowed for the operation to be established while longer-term plans were considered and established.

As Courant and other research library leaders came together, they defined what they sought to achieve not only positively but also in contrast with other major library collaborative initiatives. Two of the largest-scale not-for-profit initiatives were on the minds of many. The cataloging cooperative OCLC, for example, was technically a member-governed not-for-profit, but many librarians had long believed that it had taken on too many business practices and cultural norms of a commercial vendor. When JSTOR was established, it was governed not on the basis of membership but with an independent and self-perpetuating board of trustees, even though many of its initial staff were employees of the University of Michigan where it was first established.[35] While it was less common at the time for

---

35. Schonfeld, *JSTOR: A History.*

librarians to view JSTOR as having commercial business practices, library leaders' recent efforts to capture JSTOR's interest in the challenges and priorities facing research libraries had been equally unsuccessful.

Wilkin and others grappled with what he would call "a conundrum for our community. . . . There is a need to keep things close enough that the actors understand the needs that are being addressed. OCLC is a good example of the actors being far enough away that they don't understand. They felt we needed a well-formed record for a digital object, but we needed it connected to the print. How do we keep a knowledge of the need without getting caught in the morass of the government documents librarian who can't see their way out of the immediate problem?" The answer, he feels, is "collective ownership, keeping it close, keeping the governance close."[36]

Recognizing that any organization that charges money and grows to a large scale is often characterized as commercial rather than collaborative by the broader library community, the research library leaders working to establish HathiTrust were determined not to drift away from their needs as libraries nor to let their collaboration become "captured" over time by a third party. Beyond looking to establish a strong technical solution, they equally sought to model a form of governance that would ensure that their initiative remained a collaboration of and for academic and research libraries.

Toward this end, Hathi was organized as a subsidiary of the University of Michigan's library, which served as its financial agent, employer of many of its staff members, and infrastructural home. Indeed, its founding executive director would concurrently serve as associate university librarian for

36. Wilkin, interview.

technology and publishing, allowing for resources to be shared relatively freely as needed. Its board—responsible for governance but with Hathi operating as a wholly owned subsidiary of Michigan—was almost entirely library directors and totally controlled by CIC members: "one vote from CIC, one from California, one from Indiana, and two from Michigan." The members committed to reviewing governance models after a three-year start-up period.[37]

With its organization and leadership rooted strongly in libraries, Hathi charged a variety of committees with participation from across its membership to define and develop its services. Technical and development contributions were made by a number of members, not only Michigan.

The renewed focus on access brought an important moment for strategic definition. From its leaders' choice of name in its earliest days, it must have been clear that HathiTrust was not intended as a user-facing service. Preservation was at its heart, and it was a partnership with dozens of institutional members. Even so, it faced a variety of architectural choices about whether it would be run as a back-office infrastructure white-labeled by libraries or whether it would develop its own brand identity as a starting point. Initial plans called for white-labeling that the University of Michigan, for example, could point its users to a page like http://umich.hathitrust.org, essentially outsourcing its digital library infrastructure, which would in turn carry the university branding. But at almost this very moment, a sea change was taking place in library discovery, and university libraries were envisioning a future where, well beyond their catalog, they could provide a single easy-to-use interface

37. Wilkin, interview.

allowing for the discovery of all their collections. HathiTrust began to be seen as a larger collection in its own right and a suitable target for a library discovery service. Unfortunately, such discovery services have not, at the time of this writing, taken on a very high share of usage. Users are far more likely to encounter the content through Google Books than they are through HathiTrust, even if as a result they are searching a smaller corpus by many measures.

Organizing for Sustainability

One of the outcomes of keeping governance close was that members and potential members had many ideas about the directions that HathiTrust could take once its preliminary goals were achieved. Some saw it as a potential publishing platform for university presses and a sort of meta-institutional repository for scholarly communications offices. Some saw it as the solution to the government documents conundrum, in which many academic library leaders were looking to achieve greater collections management flexibility and escape their traditional responsibilities for these tangible collections. And there were many other ideas as well. With the initial start-up period coming to a close, Hathi's leaders looked to organize a "constitutional convention" to develop a governance structure and business model to carry the initiative forward.

Leading up to this "convention," Hathi leaders decided to commission an objective third-party report examining the progress that had been made to date and some future possibilities. The partners were reaching a point where choosing certain strategic directions, and forswearing others, might be beneficial. Up to this point, membership had grown steadily beyond the initial partners, and there were dilemmas about whether to continue the growth and if so what strategic and governance implications Hathi would likely face.[38]

The constitutional convention resulted in certain key changes in Hathi's decision-making structure and business models. Perhaps most significantly, a new pricing model was introduced, reducing the emphasis on whose digitized files were stored in the platform and increasing the emphasis on overall overlap with the library's tangible collections. This model reflected the court decisions of the time, suggesting that Hathi's value proposition was in a library's ability to withdraw a print volume in favor of electronic access, rather than through improved discoverability or access beyond public domain collections, the latter of which was not possible. Additionally, the decision-making structure was expanded to incorporate voting beyond the founding partners and to build a governing board that was more broadly representative.

Notwithstanding this change in decision-making structure, the convention resulted in no formal organizational change, such as the creation of an independent not-for-profit organization. Hathi remained in a very real sense an organ of the University of Michigan, with the executive director and other key staff members employed by its university library. This structure may have had key benefits in the context of various types of copyright litigation, since as a state body the university might have been able to assert sovereign immunity in certain circumstances. Whether this type of risk management was a principal factor in determining Hathi's organizational and governance structure, or whether it was entirely a desire

---

38. This project was conducted by one of the authors, Schonfeld, and his then Ithaka S+R colleague Matthew Loy.

for libraries not to "lose control" of another community collaboration, is not known.

Directions

So many years were spent getting HathiTrust off the ground and shaping its governance that it is important to remember just how significant an undertaking it has been. By 2018, more than one hundred libraries had joined this shared initiative, and collectively they were doing far more together than just storing digitized books. At the most basic level, they had created a preservation-worthy repository that received certification from the Center for Research Libraries under the Trustworthy Repositories Audit and Certification (TRAC) standard. Programmatic initiatives abounded. HathiTrust worked to shape the landscape for federal government documents, with the idea of allowing hundreds of depository libraries to replace their print holdings with digital availability. HathiTrust's shared print program helped libraries record commitments to retaining print materials, enabling other libraries to consider the prospect of withdrawing their copies. A research center was created under the auspices of HathiTrust to enable various kinds of sophisticated text mining and analysis of the digitized holdings. A large initiative was mounted to review the copyright status of many of the books to make as many as possible publicly accessible, far more so than were digitized through the Google initiative alone.[39] These early programmatic initiatives both opened up access to the digitized versions, for reading and analysis, and began helping libraries transform their print collections.

39. Melissa Levine et al., *Finding the Public Domain: The Copyright Review Management System* (Ithaka S+R, 2016), https://doi.org/10.18665/sr.289081.

Another important feature of the HathiTrust is that it established the HathiTrust Research Center (now jointly managed by the University of Illinois, Indiana University, and the HathiTrust) to allow computational analysis of the content held by the HathiTrust. Recognizing that scholars and researchers would likely need help when dealing with such a massive corpus, HathiTrust developed a technical infrastructure and tools that allow text mining and other forms of research. HathiTrust has funded scholarly research based on the corpus and regularly hosts workshops that encourage researchers to explore questions that can be answered by using the database.

While some in the library community wished for HathiTrust to become a kind of universal library, the organization saw itself as a shared repository, and Mike Furlough, who succeeded John Wilkin as executive director, was clear about his objective: "Part of my mission right now is getting things done that we said we would do. Google is still digitizing, though not as much. They will digitize for another couple of years, so, my short-term strategy is to get as much through that pipeline as possible, while a digitization pipeline still exists." This was vital for the library members of HathiTrust whose print collections continued to be digitized. But it was not, at least not yet, a current collection including newly published born digital materials. And so, it too fell far short of the Universal Library.[40]

Although it was a challenge building the partnership, the economics of HathiTrust seems self-evident in retrospect. Wilkin explains Hathi as a "collective collection problem. It is not an institutional problem. We want to own these things in a collective way. My institution as a partner deposits every book we digitize into HathiTrust—we don't have a local copy.

---

40. Furlough, interview.

[At UIUC] I pay $35,000 a year for infrastructure that would cost me $2 million if I created it myself. It's a simple mathematical problem. And better quality metadata, etc. And I get five million public domain volumes."[41] As a repository it is a huge success. But on some basic level, its start as a repository may also have limited its ambitions. "Hathi is a preservation strategy, but it also does more with access. Preservation is a hard foundation to build on. People pay lip service to preservation, but it is hard to get people to pay for it."[42]

41. Wilkin, interview.
42. Furlough, interview.

8

Implications

During the period we examined in this project, major advances in digitization and digital availability took humanity closer than ever before to achieving the long-standing dream of universal access to humanity's knowledge. By bringing the vast legacy of human knowledge into the digital realm, our generation could perhaps begin to reimagine its form for the future. The most ambitious digitization program was built on two fundamental ingredients: the wealth of collections that research libraries had assembled and stewarded for generations; and the vision, leadership, and monetary and engineering resources that Google brought to bear. In the end, discovery was absolutely transformed, but the outcomes went well beyond Google's initial discussion of a "digital card catalog." In addition, text mining and other transformative uses enabled entirely new categories of usage, access to public domain material skyrocketed, and a digital-first mind-set came to many libraries. But, rather than a universal digital library, we have a potpourri of digital collections, with greater or lesser access, as well as libraries that have individually become digital, more or less.

In parallel, the information environment in which the general public operates became fractured. The filter bubble became all too real. Conspiracy theory competed with reality. Authority collapsed and institutions were threatened. Validated information sourced from publications and the expertise that they held dwindled in societal significance. All this took place notwithstanding the efforts made by leading commercial online services—especially by Google, as we have profiled in this book, but also supported by Microsoft and Yahoo—to bring validated sources of information into their services.

Google's big plans to make knowledge widely accessible to all were cut short by a legal ruling, so it is not surprising that Google lost strategic interest. Digitization continued, but at a much reduced pace—and without the urgency associated with building a comprehensive digital library. Perhaps most damaging was that in-copyright materials could not be fully integrated into the online consumer discovery environment.

Librarians who had advocated for community-led initiatives to build the national library could have rallied to unify libraries in a common goal of building that library. Individual research libraries made significant progress in digitizing their collections for the convenience of their users, but coordinated efforts were elusive. Interestingly, other than Robert Darnton, who worked valiantly to galvanize the community around the Digital Public Library concept, there were no other such organized efforts. Perhaps there was no such thing as a "research library community"—but it is more likely that the budgets of individual research libraries were simply not adequate to take on massive projects with multiple partners to serve a public interest.

Google took the view that by digitizing major research libraries' collections, it would "get to scale" in building a digital library. Scholars complained that the result would not be a comprehensive digital library, but the libraries participating in the Google project argued that unfortunate gaps could be filled in at a later time. But, given the budget pressures of research libraries, will they be filled? And if so, by whom?

Even in the short period between the height of Google's book digitization efforts and today, societal views of what constitutes comprehensive knowledge have changed significantly. Through today's lens, many are now asking if the major research libraries are actually representative enough of American history, culture, and scholarship to serve as a comprehensive digital library. Earlier standards, assumptions, and biases no doubt resulted in numerous voices being omitted, which would have been reflected in the digitization initiative based on the institutions that were selected and the approach being taken. In the early part of the twenty-first century, most research libraries focused more on globalization than on deepening the range of domestic resources. It is surely the case that today's librarians will want to add resources to the digital collective that were not considered as important twenty years ago. Perhaps the implication of current thinking is that many more institutions must necessarily be involved in building a comprehensive digital library, making the budget questions even more daunting.[1]

---

1. At an individual institutional level, these efforts for collections diversification and repatriation, and improved description and classification, are often referred to as "decolonizing" the library, museum, or collection. For example, see Elisa Shoenberger, "What Does It Mean to Decolonize a Museum?" *Museum Next*, February 11, 2020, https://www.museumnext.com/article/what-does-it-mean-to-decolonize-a-museum/.

A Universal Library—Redefined

One element of our work in this book has been to determine if Google and its partner libraries could have established a universal library of the published record. By that, we mean *a single coordinated program to provide digital access for the entire intellectual and cultural record that is easy to use and ubiquitously accessible.* Notwithstanding the digitization of millions of books, their efforts toward universality were slowed by legal wrangling and mooted as a technology company pivoted with agility to the next priority. Google deserves enormous credit for making more progress than many others, not only with its book digitization program but also in related projects to support the visual arts and other sectors, but its ultimately commercial motivation probably meant it would never singlehandedly spearhead the universal library. But Google was not the only entity with an aspiration of its own, or aspirations of others projected upon it, to create a universal digital library. Though Google appeared to be the best hope for a universal library, that aspiration may have been unrealistic. If Google was not the answer, were there other non-commercial alternatives?

For a while, it seemed that the Digital Public Library of America might play the central leadership role. With the collaboration of John Palfrey, government agencies such as the Institute of Museum and Library Services (IMLS) and the National Endowment for the Humanities (NEH) as well as private funders such as the Sloan Foundation invested significant resources to launch the digital library. Robert Darnton, from the beginning of DPLA, talked about it as a free resource. While the notion of a freely accessible digital library was compelling to many, those who had responsibility for managing the organization struggled to find an appropriate business model to sustain it.

Still, DPLA made a most important contribution in articulating its fundamental principle that all cultural organizations hold collections that tell a portion of the American story, and all should be represented in a universal library that is available to everyone.

The Library of Congress could have decided that the failed settlement opened the way for national leadership. James Billington prioritized the digitization of primary source materials and the World Digital Library that featured treasures of great libraries around the globe. Under the leadership of Billington, the Library of Congress focused on the role it could play for the nation. Billington believed in the importance of federal institutions providing services for the people's tax dollars. He did not see political value in coordinating efforts with other research libraries, ensuring that scholars had a robust research library network in which to work, even though a good number of libraries across the country were hoping to be part of such a system. For making an impression on legislators, though, Billington earned far more credit for providing information resources that could be readily used by public school teachers and their students. With the appointment of Carla Hayden as Librarian of Congress in 2016, librarians applauded one of their own taking the helm and the more outward-facing leadership they anticipated she would provide. With her background as a public librarian, many expected that she would focus on greater accessibility of the collections and greater collaboration with the broad library community. Her early public statements reinforced this view: she expected the library to digitize half of its collections during the first five years of her tenure.[2] But instead of focusing on massive digitization in order to make the collections more broadly available, the national library instead has planned new exhibitions to bring visitors, more activities for children and young people, and more programs that connect people to the collections. The approach will elevate interpretation and visitorship over the deep needs of researchers, at least according to the president of the staff union.[3] The Library has also launched major initiatives to diversify its collections and collecting practices.[4] Suffice it to say that under two very different leadership models and organizational visions, the Library of Congress has been consistent in not prioritizing the kind of national coordination and leadership that would have been needed to create a more coordinated universal library.

While programmatic leadership represents one model for coordinating decentralized efforts, aggregation and discovery might be seen as an alternative approach, and certainly one that has been quite effective. ProQuest, for example, partners with thousands of publishers to aggregate books and journals in digital format, along with special collections materials that have been digitized from libraries and an array of video, data, and other materials. ProQuest and its leading competitor, EBSCO,

2. Baynard Woods, "Carla Hayden: New Librarian of Congress Makes History, with an Eye on the Future," *The Guardian*, September 15, 2016.

3. Peggy McGlone, "The Library of Congress Wants to Attract More Visitors: Will That Undermine Its Mission?" *Washington Post*, March 11, 2019, https://www .washingtonpost.com/entertainment/museums/the-library-of-congress-wants-to -attract-more-visitors-will-that-compromise-its-scholarly-mission/2019/03/07 /582d590e-1a90-11e9-8813-cb9dec761e73_story.html?utm_term=.84a4aa2fc44d.

4. For an overview, see Peggy McGlone, "Library of Congress Gets $15 Million to Diversify Partners, Collections," *Washington Post*, January 27, 2021, https://www .washingtonpost.com/entertainment/library-of-congress-diversity-grant/2021/01/26 /f4721430-5fe9-11eb-afbe-9a1a127d146_story.html.

then license access to this central aggregation (or components of it) and make it available by subscription to libraries and their users. While the aggregator model has been especially valuable in curating a collection that is more or less appropriate for undergraduate education, the needs of researchers are far more vast. And so these companies, along with OCLC, have also come to offer what are known as "discovery" services, which are based on an index of substantially all the digital resources that can be useful for scholarship, including the print holdings of research libraries, materials in institutional repositories, the vast array of e-journals, special collections materials, and much more. These discovery services offer, in essence, a more curated version of a Google search—eliminating the vast open web in favor of some kind of academically appropriate universe of content.[5]

Thus, instead of a *single coordinated program to provide digital access for the entire intellectual and cultural record that is easy to use and ubiquitously accessible*, perhaps we can imagine another model for the universal library: one that is *the accumulation of many efforts, all of them ultimately incomplete, controlled by an array of different actors*. Even without programmatic coordination, the accumulated efforts of many individuals and organizations, linked up by aggregation and especially discovery, have brought and continue to bring more information into the hands of ordinary individuals (not to mention scholars) than all but the dreamers ever could have imagined. There can be little doubt but that society is reaping enormous benefits from

5. Other new discovery services, including platforms such as Meta and Dimensions, are similarly improving the ability of a scholarly user to find materials relevant to their research, although those more focused on science tend to emphasize newer publications and provide an array of sophisticated tools to sort through and analyze the avalanche of scientific research.

the progress that has been made by technology companies, entrepreneurs, libraries, publishers, and individuals who wish to see more content made accessible. While a single, comprehensive digital library has not been realized, and programmatic leadership to coordinate decentralized efforts has been limited, there are numerous smaller successes that, in combination with a vision for aggregation and discovery, add up to transformed access to the scholarly and cultural record.

Research and Scholarship Transformed

While the Google book digitization project was but one of the factors in the digital transformation of scholarship, its importance for many fields was absolutely singular. Simply enabling the full-text search of millions of books—even just with snippet-level access—has been transformative.

Over time, humanists in particular and a variety of other academics would cite, again and again, the value of Google's initiative in improving their ability to discover works that would be important to their scholarship. In one project interviewing several dozen historians, we heard repeatedly of the singular importance of Google's digitized books. With respect to their use of Google's digitized library books, one historian explained that "being able to search for a particular word that I'm interested in is so much more powerful than searching in a library catalog. It's not in any title. It's not in a subject term. Everything in my field is out of copyright and digitized. It's all there. I feel like I'm cheating half the time."[6]

6. Jennifer Rutner and Roger C. Schonfeld, "Supporting the Changing Research Practices of Historians," *Ithaka S+R*, December 7, 2012, https://sr.ithaka.org/publications/supporting-the-changing-research-practices-of-historians/.

Indeed, this improved discovery was so transformative that Lara Putnam has pointed to a methodological revolution for certain types of historical scholarship. Speaking of an array of digitization, including the Google project, Putnam wrote:

> Increasing reach and speed by multiple orders of magnitude is transformative. It makes new realms of connection visible, new kinds of questions answerable. At the same time, the new topography of information has systematic blind spots. It opens shortcuts that enable ignorance as well as knowledge. Digital search offers release from place-based research practices that have been central to our discipline's epistemology and ethics alike.[7]

Humanists foresaw these needs and started building their own tools in parallel with early library initiatives, many of them funded by Mellon, IMLS, or NEH. This included widely distributed and well-used services like Zotero and Tropy, as well as an array of research projects using computational methods, new forms of visualization and analysis, and a variety of other techniques collectively termed "digital humanities."

The Continuing Power of Print

While scholarship was transformed in so many humanistic fields, scholars' long-form reading preferences remained with print format. Although much may have changed due to the disruption from the pandemic, as of 2018, books remained a stubbornly dual-format content type, with discovery and certain

---

7. Lara Putnam, "The Transnational and the Text-Searchable: Digitized Sources and the Shadows They Cast," *American Historical Review* 121, no. 2 (April 2016): 377–402, https://doi.org/10.1093/ahr/121.2.377.

forms of access taking place almost entirely digitally while long-form reading continued to be pursued largely with tangible codices.[8] As a consequence, key parts of the academic library collections, especially books—the tangible collections of which were digitized with Google—continued to be collected in print format even as demands for sophisticated digital tools grew as well. Not only the libraries and archives but also the publishers that enabled humanistic scholarship found the digital transformation to be quite a tricky challenge to navigate.

University presses have their greatest strengths in monographs, especially for the humanities and certain social sciences fields. While there has continued to be substantial sales pressure on monograph lists, presses like those of the universities of Michigan and California have established platforms such as Fulcrum and *Editoria* that enable them to experiment with format, and partnerships with libraries such as TOME have advanced open access models for monographs. At the same time, university presses have made inroads with crossover trade titles, the midlist that many trade publishers have abandoned, as well as regional and other specialized lists. As universities questioned the public good role of their presses and looked to manage them increasingly as businesses, many presses have been reorganized into academic libraries, and some interesting partnerships have emerged as a result. Still, regardless of organizational model, precarity is more typical than growth when looking across the sector.

Trade publishers have been shaped by a different pressure. While most of the major American publishers started as small, family-owned businesses that had close ties to the authors they

8. Melissa Blankstein and Christine Wolff-Eisenberg, "Ithaka S+R US Faculty Survey 2018," *Ithaka S+R*, 2019, https://doi.org/10.18665/sr.311199.

represented, mergers and acquisitions in the last half of the twentieth century resulted in many of these small publishing houses being bought by large telecommunications or entertainment companies or even by large conglomerates that were not strategically focused on publishing. Books have become relatively less important to many as other forms of entertainment such as streaming media and games command a greater share of leisure time. And changes in the distribution landscape, including the erosion of independent bookstores, the transition to e-books, and the growth of audio books, have strengthened Amazon as an intermediary.

Optimizing Print Collections

Tangible collections of printed books now were needed largely for long-form reading alone, with browsing and index-based consultation largely addressed digitally. Facing a strategic imperative to address digital needs and the scientific, medical, and professional fields that were increasingly important to their universities, libraries began to seek opportunities to "optimize" their print collections, "managing down" collections that had been developed for an era when digital search and online access were not available.[9] This would require a vast rethinking of how collections are organized, housed, preserved, and shared—and who pays for these functions of supplying print. Academic libraries have recognized for more than a decade that large-scale change is not only possible but, in the view of some, needed. At the same time, some scholars have expressed

---

9. See, for example, Lorcan Dempsey's work on "managing down" print collections: https://www.lorcandempsey.net/orweblog/managing-down-collections/.

significant concern that, in dismantling existing collections, library leaders could impede certain research methods.[10] The changes in library collaboration, technology systems, and even organizational structure and staffing needed to advance this agenda have been slower to develop.[11] Recent commitments to create a single shared collection across the Big Ten academic libraries, if pursued, would represent a remarkable step forward.[12]

But while library leaders circled around these problems, others overlooked the nuances. With more and more content being found with a few keystrokes in the Google search box, more university and college administrators, not to mention trustees, began to take note of the large budget for the campus library. Many asked if Google would not replace the library. Wouldn't everything be online for students to use? Why did books need to be cataloged and assigned subject headings when a word search in Google yielded useful results? And many administrators saw ways to reduce institutional budgets by relying more on the free resources of Google rather than continuing to build massive print collections locally.

Librarians saw great promise in digital technology, but funding digital library development was challenging. Many librarians hoped to secure additional funds beyond those allocated

10. See, for example, Andrew M. Stauffer, *Book Traces: Nineteenth-Century Readers and the Future of the Library* (Philadelphia: University of Pennsylvania Press, 2021).

11. Gwen Evans and Roger Schonfeld, *It's Not What Libraries Hold; It's Who Libraries Serve: Seeking a User-Centered Future for Academic Libraries* (New York: Ithaka S+R, 2020), https://doi.org/10.18665/sr.312608.

12. Lindsay Ellis, "The Future of Campus Libraries? 'Sticky Interdependence,'" *Chronicle of Higher Education*, October 9, 2019, https://www.chronicle.com/article/The-Future-of-Campus/247323.

for print materials for developing and sustaining the digital library. They were already planning for a future in which digitized collections would allow them to provide more advanced services, going far beyond local collections. As administrators considered reducing budgets through greater reliance on digital resources, librarians thought of digital resources largely in addition to their legacy print collections.

Virtually all academic libraries recognized that in the digital environment, users expected to have access to resources well beyond those contained within the walls of the local library. They began to prioritize services they could offer to provide broader, more convenient access over developing local collections. They also were forced to develop digital tools and services for students and faculty, since the users no longer needed to be in the physical space to take advantage of the libraries' offerings. Librarians who had been responsible for providing on-site reference services became "embedded" librarians who moved out of the library building to work directly with faculty in their departments and programs.

Library Collaboration

Many academic library leaders came to believe that the best path forward for their work was to achieve cross-institutional scale for a variety of new digital services and collaborations to help them manage down print collections. During the era discussed in this book, numerous library collaborations were developed, many of them based on membership models of one sort or another. Some of these initiatives were sustained, while others were quickly wound down.

In terms of print collections management, a number of initiatives were developed, including Scholar's Trust in the

Southeast, the WEST collaboration, and the Partnership for Shared Book Collections. While their long-term sustainability is not uniformly clear,[13] they provide the basis for new models of managing print collaboratively more than institutionally.

In 2018, the library community saw a sizable number of consolidations, mergers, and closures of national-level digital initiatives. The Digital Public Library of America reduced its staff significantly because of financial concerns.[14] The Digital Preservation Network closed its doors when it became clear that the membership model would not yield sufficient revenue to keep the program going.[15] Other organizations sought to form partnerships that result in more efficient and financially viable business models.[16]

It is against this context that we should understand HathiTrust, the aggregation of books and other library materials that have been digitized by Google, the Internet Archive, or local institutions that, as of the end of 2020, numbered nearly 17.5 million volumes. Full-text viewing is available for 6.8 million public domain volumes. Paul Courant's extraordinary foresight must be acknowledged here. When Google approached the University of Michigan about digitizing its library collection, Google had not thought of providing the university with a copy of the digital files. Other institutions did not require

13. Schonfeld, "Taking Stock."

14. Roger C. Schonfeld, "Learning Lessons from DPLA," *Scholarly Kitchen*, November 13, 2018, https://scholarlykitchen.sspnet.org/2018/11/13/learning-lessons-from-dpla/.

15. Roger C. Schonfeld, "Why Is the Digital Preservation Network Disbanding?" *Scholarly Kitchen*, December 13, 2018, https://scholarlykitchen.sspnet.org/2018/12/13/digital-preservation-network-disband/.

16. Roger C. Schonfeld, "Restructuring Library Collaboration: Strategy, Membership, Governance," *Ithaka S+R*, March 6, 2019, https://sr.ithaka.org/publications/restructuring-library-collaboration/.

digital copies of the digitized books, as they did not know how they would store and manage such large files. Courant may not have known exactly how his institution would manage these massive files, but he fully recognized that ownership would be necessary if anything were to be done with the files later on. He sought to preserve the institution's ownership of the content it had collected, something he believed served the university's long-term interests. Rather than being developed as an independent organization, Hathi remained an operating unit of the University of Michigan, enabling it to rely on the university's infrastructure at key moments. And rather than a flat membership fee, Hathi crafted a pricing model that was designed to align participation fees with value. As a result of these important choices, Hathi has built a strong partnership that has the potential to become an increasingly comprehensive digital library. The key to this outcome would be a commitment to collective governance of a national asset rather than equity of services for individual members.

Scientific Communications

While so much bandwidth went to thinking and rethinking collections for humanists, these were a declining share of budget activity for many research libraries. By contrast, the issues for the collections necessary to support academic science were far simpler, requiring only money. In some respects, the transformation was straightforward: many academic and research libraries reallocated vast portions of their science acquisitions budgets from print purchases to digital licenses. There, the reading experience for journals had transitioned away from print versions, and so journals quickly began to be published and "collected" almost exclusively in digital form.

Major scientific publishers, such as Elsevier and IEEE, rapidly transitioned their businesses to principally digital, as print journals became a comparatively marginal business. Digital brought lower marginal costs and accelerated demands for open access to the scientific literature, along with an explosion in piracy. Some libraries demanded a shift in the publishers' businesses away from a library-side payment for the ability to read the publications toward an author payment (typically grant-funded) in order to publish an article. Publishers increasingly adopted this model, with unsettled outcomes for value and profitability. In parallel, the major scientific publishers began a series of pushes to support preprints and research data, in an effort to bolster the value of their workflows and brands, along with other tools and analytics.[17] While we write before this transformation can be said to have been completed, the direction of travel is well established.

Digital Reflections

The digitization of library collections enabled and reflected a broader directional shift from print to digital production and sales of scholarly and, to some extent, trade publications. These shifts enabled digital offerings to be made available through both consumer sales channels and library sales channels, with the latter enabling academic libraries to transition their acquisitions to digital form as rapidly as readership and budget would support. Both journal and book publishers confronted the reality that the convenience and ease of access afforded by digital

---

17. See Danielle Cooper, Oya Y. Rieger, and Roger C. Schonfeld, "Can Publishers Maintain Control of the Scholarly Record?" *Scholarly Kitchen*, January 6, 2021, https://scholarlykitchen.sspnet.org/2021/01/06/can-publishers-control-scholarly-record/.

publishing would forever change the reading preferences and habits of scholars and students alike. At the same time, Google's involvement in book digitization showed the agility and capital that commercial technology firms could bring to bear in this space, and the commercial scholarly publishers took note as they transformed themselves into technology and data powerhouses.

Although we have focused on many of the less-than-perfect attempts to create a comprehensive digital library, it is also important to acknowledge the significant progress that has been achieved. By 2020, technology has become a key ingredient of scholarship, publishers have found many more ways of making their content available to users, and libraries have become increasingly digital. The open access movement has resulted in new business models for publishing. Libraries and publishers alike, with a combination of grant and institutional funds, have made great progress in making more resources available to ever-widening audiences. Google did not complete its aspiration to build a universal library, but after Google's book digitization project came along, libraries, publishers, scholars, and innovators all took notice, and their accomplishments toward creating greater access to the world's knowledge are laudable.

Epilogue

In writing this book, we have been surprised by the degree to which change has occurred in higher education, and especially in scholarly communication. Technological innovation, online learning in institutions of higher education, open access, and ubiquitous "self publishing" have dramatically altered the system of scholarly communication as we knew it at the end of the twentieth century.

Even though evangelists of progress complain about the reluctance of publishing houses to change, there has been a remarkable transition to digital in the last couple of decades. The willingness of philanthropic organizations such as the Andrew W. Mellon Foundation and the Albert P. Sloan Foundation, and federal funding agencies NEH and IMLS, to fund experimental digital scholarship has accelerated the acceptance of new types of scholarly works, and the ingenuity of some of them is breathtaking. Beginning with Edward Ayers's "Valley of the Shadow" project in 1993, humanists found ways to create non-linear interactive tools that could be used to interrogate the databases that humanists created by other scholars and the general public as well. In the sciences, projects such as the Sloan Digital Sky Survey, started in 2000, have resulted in petabytes of data being open to all researchers for analysis. Blogs and social media posts have become important sources of scholarly information in all fields. Publishers developed search capabilities for users that did not require an intermediary as well, and they made the discovery process easier and more relevant by developing researcher-centric platforms for accessing their materials.

With vast quantities of scholarly information being readily available online, it appeared that the library was becoming a less important organization as a repository of knowledge. So much could be discovered through electronic devices at home. Smaller academic institutions, and even some of the larger ones, began to question the need for the book storehouse function of the library, noting that the books were rarely consulted. Large research libraries, through consortia, banded together to create a single repository for little-used books. Through one collection, all have access when it is needed. Smaller colleges have moved books out of their libraries, either to off-site storage facilities or into the dumpster, to make space for other units of the institution that support student success: academic advising, writing centers, or computer labs. College librarians note that nearly all of the needs of their students are met through licensed access to scholarly databases.

Those assumptions about the future of libraries that were aiming toward an electronic future were accelerated dramatically as we were finishing this manuscript. So many things changed when the coronavirus pandemic found its way to the United States in 2020. Universities, libraries, restaurants, and businesses were shuttered for weeks and only slowly reopened; travel came to a standstill; schools were closed for many months. Hospitals were stretched to the breaking point. Everyone who could do so worked from home, and the videoconferencing platform Zoom became ubiquitous. Physical distancing and face masks quickly became social norms.

At a basic human level, the pandemic stoked fear and heartbreak, but when viewed through a lens of scholarly communication, the new landscape is breathtaking. Faculty members in every institution of higher learning learned to use the technology to teach their classes online in a matter of two weeks. In institutions that had developed the infrastructure for online learning, even where faculty adoption had been slow, the switch was turned on immediately after spring break and that was the sole delivery medium for instruction for the thousands of students who had been sent home for the remainder of the academic term. Families learned to allocate computer time to adults working from home, college students who had returned home, and K–12 students whose days were now structured by online classes.

Employees of all types of organizations learned that they could continue their work by adopting technology to bring people together for meetings and planning sessions. Calendars that were once full of in-person meetings quickly filled up with Zoom or Go to Meeting sessions. Committees continued to meet, candidate searches moved to virtual interviews, and the IT help desks were kept busy teaching everyone how to use the new platforms effectively.

Although library buildings were closed, their services were urgently needed by faculty members and students alike who were forced to adapt to online teaching and learning. Students at a distance forced librarians to adapt equally quickly to providing online services to students and researchers. They helped faculty members adapt their classes to online delivery. They identified high-quality resources that students could use no matter where they were located. They helped students navigate using learning management systems most effectively, and they found new ways to deliver assistance virtually.

The entire world confronted a new phenomenon, and while scientists turned their full attention to understanding the nature of a new and deadly virus, libraries, publishers, and scholarly societies recognized that they held information that might prove to be useful in the urgent research effort. An amazing number of content stewards announced that they would remove any barriers to access to their materials, and it was not only scientific studies that were included. Recognizing that students now working from home needed materials to complete their assignments, they made their resources available. Museums and art galleries—even zoos—created online exhibitions and virtual tours. Magazine publishers offered virtual tours of gardens, vacation spots, and archaeological sites.

In this moment, HathiTrust came to play a vital role. Asserting fair use, it announced an Emergency Temporary Access Service, designed to provide access to the digitized versions of tangible materials that were suddenly physically inaccessible in its member libraries. By possessing a copy of the scanned books, the member libraries were able to launch an urgently needed service almost immediately. Even though he could not have foreseen the specifics, HathiTrust member libraries were well prepared for this challenging moment because of Courant's original vision and their ongoing collective infrastructure investment.[1]

1. See Roger C. Schonfeld, "Research Library Digitization Has Found Its Moment: Long-Term Investments Pay Off and Provide Lessons for the Future," *Ithaka S+R,*

Brewster Kahle, the entrepreneurial risk-taker who had worked hard to make web resources freely available in the era of the Google digitization effort, while also taking pride in avoiding court cases, took yet another risk in the wake of the pandemic. He already had a "controlled digital lending" program much like the one that HathiTrust announced. Pushing things further, the Internet Archive announced that the digital lending policy that allowed one user at a time to borrow a digitized book would be suspended and replaced with a National Emergency Library, making 1.4 million digitized books available to users at a time when schools, universities, and libraries were closed. Kahle used the justification that "today, there are 650 million books that tax-paying citizens have paid to access that are sitting on shelves in closed libraries, inaccessible to them. And that's just in public libraries."[2]

As Kahle predicted, both the Authors Guild and the Association of American Publishers issued statements condemning the Internet Archive for robbing authors of royalties by making digitized resources universally accessible. Kahle made the same argument that publishers and vendors and cultural organizations made as they released previously locked resources available: we are in a crisis and freely available information is a much-needed public good. On June 1, 2020, John Wiley & Sons, Hachette Book Group, HarperCollins, and Penguin Random House filed suit in federal court to block the operations of the Internet Archive and to recover damages from copyright

April 21, 2020, https://sr.ithaka.org/blog/research-library-digitization-has-found-its-moment/.

2. https://blog.archive.org/2020/03/30/internet-archive-responds-why-we-released-the-national-emergency-library/.

infringement. It felt as if the old questions from the Google suit were with us once more.

Despite the familiarity of the legal challenges, there had been tremendous progress in methods of scholarly communication. Google and the libraries that joined with it made vital contributions to the creation of a new kind of "universal library," radically expanding access to the published literature. From our vantage point in mid-2021, it is impossible to fully grasp the long-term implications of this choice.

The libraries may have made the best choice given the options available to them, but the nature of the partnership was known to be imperfect from its inception. Will we look back on this story as one in which universities and their libraries gave up control of many of their greatest intellectual assets or as one in which they made a gift of unprecedented generosity to the commons?

Ultimately, the test will lie not in the strength of libraries as organizations but rather in the strength of the intellectual authority and intellectual freedom for which they as institutions were charged with societal responsibility. It is not clear that new generations will be able to distinguish trustworthy knowledge from misinformation. Libraries have yet to demonstrate that they are prepared to sustain and protect this new kind of "universal library" from those with ill intentions. The current system of local funding for libraries makes it difficult to justify large expenditures to address national problems. While there are encouraging steps toward safeguarding the scientific and cultural record, the models for developing and maintaining its authority while making that record ever more widely available remain elusive. If these broad issues can be addressed effectively and in coordinated fashion, then the digitization bargain will have proved to be a grand success.

INDEX

A NOTE ON THE TYPE

This book has been composed in Adobe Text and Gotham. Adobe Text, designed by Robert Slimbach for Adobe, bridges the gap between fifteenth- and sixteenth-century calligraphic and eighteenth-century Modern styles. Gotham, inspired by New York street signs, was designed by Tobias Frere-Jones for Hoefler & Co.